THE WORSHIP OF GOD

IS VOLUME

16

OF THE

Twentieth Century Encyclopedia of Catholicism

UNDER SECTION

II

THE BASIC TRUTHS

IT IS ALSO THE

26TH

VOLUME IN ORDER OF PUBLICATION

Edited by HENRI DANIEL-ROPS of the Académie Française

THE WORSHIP OF GOD

By M.-D. PHILIPPE, O.P.

Translated from the French by DOM MARK PONTIFEX

HAWTHORN BOOKS · PUBLISHERS · New York

First Edition, September, 1959

NIHIL OBSTAT

Hubertus Richards, S.T.L., L.S.S.

Censor Deputatus

IMPRIMATUR

E. Morrogh Bernard

Vicarius Generalis

Westmonasterii, die XXVII MAII MCMLIX

CONTENTS

INTRODUCTION

Only in so far as he recognizes his Creator's sovereign rights over him can man fully realize his own nature. If he does not discover God, and does not recognize God's rights, but looks at himself as his own master, he fails to discover the source and object of his being, and then he is like a traveller who has lost his way, knowing neither where he comes from nor where he is going to.

That is why God attaches such importance in his training of mankind to the revelation of his mystery, and to the first commandment which enjoins worship. For it is by means of worship that man recognizes his absolute dependence upon God, and enters into personal relations with his Creator and his Father, comes into his presence, and gains a practical knowledge of the goodness and sovereign majesty of his God.

Once man forgets the claim of his first commandment, and allows himself to be carried away by sensible good, by ambition for worldly glory and power, his personality dwindles and loses its true nobility. Instead of aiming at the knowledge and love of God, and thereby at gaining a godlike character, man then turns back on himself, and seeks only to know and love himself. He supposes that man's true greatness consists, not in aiming at a God who is distant, "hypothetical" and even perhaps purely "imaginary," but in serving his fellow men, in loving and helping them and forgetting himself for their sakes. He supposes that true religion consists, not in adoring an unknown God, but in devoting himself to the well-being of his brethren, and drawing them closer together. We must recognize that such a "substitution" (putting man in the place of God, turning the worship of God into a means for social betterment) may be extremely attractive to one who has ceased to know what God is, or has never known, or at least has but a faint memory of it, and pictures God vaguely as an object of fear, a master always ready to punish. Such a "substitution" is surely nothing but a wicked degradation of what is holiest in the Christian mystery. Beside the cross Mary, the woman, the Mother of mankind, took John in the place of Jesus. She was to receive him as a mother, to help him, to dwell with him, to give up, we may almost say, her pure silent worship. This ultimate union of love, which the Father brought about beside the cross between the Mother of his Son and John, was indeed a union achieved through the double observance of a single commandment: to love God, to love our neighbour, to love God in our brother, and our brother for God's sake, to recognize Jesus in his members, and to love them with that same love which is reserved for Jesus. Thus, to the believer there was no substitution brought about beside the cross, since man was not put in the place of God, but God raised man to himself, and presented him to us as *his own:* "When you did it to one of the least of my brethren here, you did it to me."

The act of worship is not abolished to make way for a mere service of mankind, but God makes use of a worship which is silent, hidden and spiritual, to allow men to love one another more, to unite them in the bonds of a closer love, uniting the mother to the son, the son to the mother. That is the loving service which religion ordains, and which should be practised by the members of Christ, in the new humanity, purchased with Christ's blood. The jealous pride of the devil cannot endure such an exaltation of mankind. He seeks by every means to disfigure this new union of the cross, and to offer us a seductive caricature, which puts the cross far away from us: God is dead, men have slain God, they must now take the place of God, they must shake off the tyrannical slavery of religion, which makes them acknowledge themselves as creatures of God. They must become aware of their own sovereignty, of their own absolute freedom; true religion should be philanthropic; man saves himself, and saves his brethren. The Christian, however, instead of seeking for a new world, seduced by this "new religion," this discovery of the new greatness of man, must understand with a new clearness the act of worship he performs so often but so imperfectly. Faced with the false mysticism of the super-man, who is raised above all, the Christian must understand that more than ever he should, in the name of all humanity, worship his God, the Creator and Father of all life.

The Christian should be convinced that this is the most effective, indeed the only entirely effective, answer that he can give to his brethren who have rejected God, and do not wish to hear about God.

God himself tells us this, and teaches it with the greatest emphasis in the Old Testament, when the people of Israel in Egypt, under the yoke of Pharaoh (the Pharaohs are good representatives of the power of purely human efforts), allowed themselves to be seduced by prosperity, riches, material abundance and earthly glory. They then forgot that they were called by God. God had called them and chosen them to be his people, to witness before all other nations that the Lord is the only God.

God wished to snatch them from this tyranny; he could not suffer the misery and forgetfulness of his people. Then he revealed himself to Moses, and told him what he willed: "I have not been blind to their complaints about the cruelty of the men who are in charge of their work. I

know what their sufferings are, and I have come down to
rescue them from the power of the Egyptians, to take
them away into a fruitful land and large, a land that is all
milk and honey" (Exod. 3. 7–8).

It was by the worship in the desert that the Lord wished
to train his people once again, to bring them back to himself and to teach them their calling. Long contact with the
riches and power of the Egyptians had turned Israel away
from its God. In spite of this the Lord watched over his
people and, in order to reawaken them to the truth, he
wished to lead them into the desert and there, by means
of worship, to set them face to face with their God, to
teach them to come into his presence.

Worship, then, is a voluntary act by which the creature
freely and deliberately recognizes all the rights of God the
Creator over it. In worship it recognizes that God is at the
source of all that it is, that all that it is depends ultimately
on God, and is derived from him, that the creature's whole
life is subject to him, and that he alone has the power of
life and death, since he is the author of life.

By means of worship the rational creature disappears
before the face of God, recognizing that before the supreme majesty of the Creator he is nothing at all, and
knowing that he is not worthy to present himself alive before God: "mortal man cannot see me, and live to tell of
it," Scripture says. That, then, is what worship brings
about; it makes us die to ourselves in order to proclaim
that God is first—the Lord God must be served first. That
is why it is by and through worship alone that the rational
creature truly presents himself before God, recognizing
his incapacity to speak to him and address him, unless
God raises him and draws him on.

Thus worship shows plainly the gulf which exists between God and the creature. It is the act which teaches
man in the most effective and emphatic way the mystery

of God's transcendence, of his sovereign majesty. The worshipper must have a deep realization that man thereby discovers not only his absolute, vital dependence on his Creator, but also his Creator's great mercy, and real love, for in worship this discovery is made by way of love. The purely speculative discovery of the philosopher that he is wholly dependent in the order of being, that in his own existence not-being comes first, is always liable to cause him distress, because it is not wholly spiritual, and the imagination may suddenly intervene. This distress then continues deep in his mind, preventing him from thinking freely, and contemplating him who is the source of light. The distress easily changes into an attitude of complete hostility and refusal. Poor human understanding cannot live in the air at such a height. This trouble—due both to metaphysics and to the imagination—may often be at the root of some bitter forms of atheism.[1]

On the other hand, in the free and voluntary act of worship, God never appears as a rival or as a tyrant who crushes us and holds us in slavery, but as the Father in the highest sense, the Creator from whom come all light, love and life. In the act of worship man recognizes the sovereign majesty of his God and Creator, the loving presence of his almighty Father, without seeing him or knowing him perfectly. Yet he is sure that he is addressing a living being who sees into the depths of his heart, and is no stranger whom he does not know. Man's act of worship of God when God is not seen may be compared to the action of a child who, having its eyes still closed and

---

[1] We must never forget that, when dealing with realities above us and beyond us, we can never know them as they really are unless we love them. Only a loving knowledge allows us to approach them sympathetically, and understand them as they are. Otherwise, we are always liable to underrate them, diminishing them to fit our own stature. Hence we can only know God perfectly through worship.

not having yet seen its mother's face, turns towards her who can tend it, feed it, warm it and protect it. There is indeed a spiritual instinct which turns man's heart and mind towards him who alone can tend and protect him, but this spiritual instinct needs to open out into a knowledge and free choice, which becomes ever clearer.

If the worship of God is not contemplation of God, nevertheless there is no contradiction between them.[2] In the normal course worship of God should open out into contemplation of God; it should be the approach to contemplation, to the intimate knowledge of God. The man who really worships God must seek to know him more and more, as deeply as he possibly can. This knowledge will bring about a worship that is more perfect, loving and free. That is why worship plays an essential part in God's training of man, since it rouses in man a profound sense of the greatness of his God and Creator, of God's sovereign majesty and of the depths of his being. The first commandment is not to know God, but to worship him.

To obtain a better grasp of the importance and excellence of worship, and of the way in which it should lead us to an intimate knowledge of God's mystery, we may first consider the great acts of worship which are described in the Old Testament. These great acts take place in sacrifices, since sacrifice as such is nothing else than the worship of the whole man, body and soul, king of the universe, recognizing officially the sovereign rights of God

---

[2] Worship, which is based on the virtue of religion, is in some sense a matter of justice. Contemplation, which is based on wisdom, the gift of wisdom, is a matter of charity, friendship with God. It would be very interesting to analyse the precise connection between justice and friendship in human life, in order to show by analogy the relation between worship and contemplation. There can be no friendship without justice, no true contemplation without worship. Friendship is the final end of justice, contemplation of worship.

over him, over his goods, all his conduct, and covering every relation in which he stands.

The acts of worship in the great Old Testament sacrifices are privileged meeting places between man and God. Each of the different sacrifices expresses a particular aspect of worship, and prefigures the great sacrifice of Christ on the cross. It is indeed Christ on the cross who alone reveals to us the mystery of worship in its entirety, and at the same time reveals, in an ultimate way, the whole mystery of God as Love.

We shall see, then, in the first chapter of this book the worship offered in the great Old Testament sacrifices, which prefigure the worship of the unique sacrifice; in the second, we shall try to examine thoroughly the loving worship of this unique sacrifice; finally, in the third chapter, in the light of Christ crucified, we shall try to see how this worship gives us a better understanding of God's mystery, of its characteristics and divine perfection. The worship of the Cross is the royal way to the contemplation of God's mystery.

CHAPTER I

THE OLD TESTAMENT SACRIFICES: TYPES OF THE SACRIFICE OF THE CROSS

SACRIFICES BEFORE THE LAW

The sacrifice of Abel

The first action of the children of Adam and Eve, of which Scripture tells us, is one of offering: "Cain brought the Lord an offering out of the crops the land had given him; Abel, too, brought an offering, and his offering was out of the first-born of his flock" (Gen. 4. 3–4). That is a most natural action for man to perform: he offers to the Lord the fruit of his labour, thereby recognizing that God is the sovereign master of the fertility of the earth and of animals.

In the case of Abel this simple action was the expression of a deep conviction, colouring his whole life. For him this offering was the recognition of God's absolute rights over his goods and over himself, and only intended to proclaim the glory of his God, the one important thing in his eyes. Hence, in making this offering, he looked only to

God, without thinking of his brother or of his brother's conduct, and without troubling himself about the way in which he approached God. Abel was a man of absolute sincerity; when he offered the first-born of his flock to God, this outward action corresponded to the inner intention of his soul, for he recognized the sovereign rights of God over the fertility of life. In sacrificing to God the first-born of his flock his soul offered itself to God; it hid itself in the majesty of its God, and desired only to concern itself with its God's sovereign greatness. Scripture tells us this in a veiled form, with the greatest simplicity, but plainly enough, when we compare the Lord's attitude to Abel with his attitude to Cain: "On Abel, and on his offering, the Lord looked with favour, but not upon Cain, or his offering." In the anthropomorphic language of Scripture it is easy to see that Abel looked to the Lord beyond the offering he made to him; the offering was a means of coming into the presence of God. Cain, on the other hand, only performed the external action of offering; he did not look to the Lord, but, being jealous of his brother, he spied upon him, his heart was turned away from God and turned wholly to his brother, not from brotherly care, but from envy and jealousy; he could not endure that his younger brother should be so attentive to God, and so attracted by him, and this annoyed and grieved him.

In spite of the rebuke given him by the Lord, in spite of his conscience which told him that such grief was wrong (it was not right for him to grieve at the happiness of his brother, at the care with which God treated younger sons, to be angry with his brother because he had done his duty, as he saw it in all sincerity), Cain let himself be carried away with anger and jealousy. The presence of his brother became increasingly unendurable. The only possible means of satisfying his jealousy was to get rid of him, to murder him.

It was jealousy against a brother in a matter of religion

which provoked the first murderer, the first fratricide. His jealousy, leading to murder, shows us clearly the completeness of Abel's offering: it affected his whole life. By declaring that God was the master of the fertility of his flocks, he recognized that God had the fullest rights over his life, and that he belonged to God. Hence he put everything in his hands, and surrendered himself to him with such simplicity. Such an act of worship has an absolute character, for it binds man to him who is his Creator, and at the same time separates him from all that is not his God.

In attacking Abel, who worshipped his God, Cain made a direct attack on God, for he who worships God is wrapped in God's sovereign majesty. God is his refuge. Cain, having failed to recognize in his heart God's absolute right over him by true worship, was unable to listen to God when he wished to correct him, though he was to be forced to recognize God's rights and submit to them. The anger of the Lord fell upon him. Cain, having failed to recognize with all sincerity that the fertility of the earth comes from God, had to recognize the curse of the earth: "Till that ground, and it will yield thee its fruit no longer; thou shalt be a wanderer, a fugitive on earth." Undergoing this punishment he learnt to recognize the absolute authority of God who is the Creator. This first offering of worship proclaimed God as master of the fertility of the earth and of living things.

In contradiction to this first act, which had its source in the heart of man and rose towards God, we are shown the devil's first caricature of worship. Outwardly all was perfect, but the intention in the heart did not correspond with the outward action of offering. Outwardly there was a gift, an offering, but inwardly there was fierce jealousy, and desire to rule: we cannot worship God if we do not love our brother, as our Lord emphatically declares (Matt. 5. 23–4).

Noah's sacrifice after the flood

"And now God found that earth was full of men's iniquities, and that the whole frame of their thought was set continually on evil; and he repented of having made men on the earth at all. So, smitten with grief to the depths of his heart, he said, I will blot out mankind, my creature, from the face of the earth. . . . Only on Noah did God look with favour" (Gen. 6. 5–8).

We know how, by means of the flood, God carried out his plan "to blot out mankind from the face of the earth," and how, by building an ark, he protected Noah. After the flood God ordered Noah to come out of the ark, and Noah's first act was to build an altar to the Lord:

> Thereupon Noah built an altar to the Lord, and chose out beasts that were clean and birds that were clean, and made burnt-offerings there. And the Lord, smelling such a scent as pleased him, made the resolve, Never again will I plague the earth on man's account, that has all the thoughts and imaginations of his heart, even in youth, so bent towards evil; never again will I send afflction such as this upon all living creatures. While the earth stands, seed-time and harvest, cold and heat, summer and winter, day and night shall keep their course unaltered. (Gen. 8. 20–22.)

This sacrifice of thanksgiving, made immediately after the flood, though already more reflective, more religious than the two first, with the construction of the altar and the distinction of clean animals, still appears as a very natural act of man, and of the head of human society. It was the first answer which Noah gave to his God and Saviour, when God returned to him the land after having cleansed it. Having escaped the danger of death man thanked God for his providential assistance, his brotherly help, while also acknowledging the justice of his anger and punishment. The sacrifice of Noah was no longer the simple act of offering, of worship, of the creature who recognizes the sovereign rights of the Creator; it was an act of thanksgiving and reparation, acknowledging that God's action was to be praised, that it was full of wisdom, justice and mercy.

The sacrifice of Noah, the new head of the human society, was all-embracing. It was the whole living world, the whole world cleansed by God, which was offered to God and accepted by him; we see this clearly from the answer God gave: "The Lord, smelling such a scent as pleased him, made the resolve, Never again will I plague the earth on man's account."

Recognition of this kind always touches God's heart profoundly, and God replied to the sacrifice of thanksgiving by a covenant which embraced the whole physical world: "While the earth stands, seed-time and harvest, cold and heat . . . shall keep their course unaltered." It was a covenant of fertility and peace: God blessed Noah and his children, and said to them:

> Increase and multiply, and fill the earth. All the beasts of earth, and the winged things of the sky, and the creeping things of earth, are to go in fear and dread of you, and I give you dominion over all the fishes of the sea. This creation that lives and moves is to provide food for you; I make it all over to you, by the same title as the herds that have growth. Only you must not eat the flesh with the blood still in it. The shedder of your own life-blood shall be held to account for it, whether man or beast; whoever takes the life of his brother-man shall answer for it to me. Man was made in God's image, and whoever sheds a man's blood must shed his own blood in return. (Gen. 9.6.)
>
> Here is a covenant I will observe with you. . . . Never more will the living creation be destroyed by the waters of a flood. . . . This, God said, shall be the pledge of the promise I am making to you, and to all living creatures, your companions, eternally; I will set my bow in the clouds (Gen. 9. 9–13).

While giving to man such general power over all living beings God reminded him of the nobility of his nature:

he is an image of God. God, while promising man that he would never repeat the flood, gave man a sign of peace, so that he might not forget the peaceful covenant that God had made with mankind and with the world. This covenant demanded a greater faithfulness from man, for God put more trust in him, leaving him a greater responsibility.

By this sacrifice of thanksgiving, by this worship which involved recognition of him, God joined man more fully with himself in his rule, leaving to man's care the government of the world, while reminding him that man "has all the thoughts and imagination of his heart, even in youth, so bent towards evil" (Gen. 8. 21).

The sacrifice of Isaac

The sacrifices of Abel and of Noah were real archetypes, having in some sense a universal application, actions which expressed a religious attitude, the attitude of a man who is naturally and supernaturally directed towards God, and puts all his trust in God. Abel, set aside by his brother, found in God his refuge; Noah, worshipping God, thanking him for his protection, was called by God to live in peace, to make a covenant, with him.

With Abraham, however, the history of the people of Israel begins, starting with the summons freely made by God, an imperative call to him to leave his land, a summons full of trust and promising to make of him a great people. This was a wonderful declaration on God's part, and Abraham submitted in silence, carrying out God's command.

Having chosen him God gradually revealed himself to him, showing himself to him, blessing him, making a covenant with him, while Abraham replied by building altars to God, recognizing him as God, as having full rights over him.

From the standpoint we are adopting one fact governs all the personal relations uniting the Lord with him whom he had chosen. After the birth of Isaac, which he had looked forward to with such hope, and which came about in so wonderful a way, when Abraham was filled with joy and pride, God then wished to prove him. "After this, God would put Abraham to the test," we are told by Scripture. "So he called to him, Abraham, Abraham; and when he said, I am here, at thy command, God told him, Take thy only son Isaac, with thee, to the land of Clear Vision, and there offer him to me in burnt-sacrifice on a mountain which I will shew thee." Abraham rose at once (Gen. 22. 1–3).

This time it is God who takes the first step, who demands this sacrifice to prove the fidelity of his servant and friend. It is God who himself decides the material for the holocaust, and when it shall be carried out. After having loaded Abraham with favours, and having given him this child and promised him so much, God demands an offering of all he possesses. God insists, with apparent cruelty, "take thy only son, thy beloved son Isaac." God requires that the father shall sacrifice his beloved son as a holocaust, to show his love, beyond all else, for him, the Lord. God requires that for his sake Abraham shall destroy what he has freely given him, the gift which was the special sign of his love. He demands it in order to probe Abraham's heart, to see how far he can trust him.

To human reason there appears to be a kind of contradiction in God's conduct, for it is not merely a question of his giving and taking back, but of giving after having intensified the desire, by promising, partially fulfilling, promising again and finally fulfilling by an almost miraculous gift. It is indeed a question of giving with all the generosity of a sovereign God, then of demanding from those who were favoured by the gift its total destruction, that they might declare by this destruction the sovereign rights of the giver.

However terrible might be the demands of God, Abraham, as a faithful servant, obeyed at once; he rose up quickly. He set out to fulfil God's order completely. Such was his faith that he did not hesitate for an instant to accept God's word. Without discussion he submitted to the conditions of the sacrifice. He submitted to the worship of God in the way desired by God himself, acknowledged his sovereign, absolute rights. Scripture describes this with remarkable restraint:

> He cut the wood needed for the burnt-sacrifice, and then set out for the place of which God had spoken to him. It was two days later when he looked up and saw it, still far off; and now he said to his servants, Wait here with the ass, while I and my son make our way yonder; we will come back to you, when we have offered worship there. Then he took the wood for the sacrifice, and gave it to his son Isaac to carry; he himself carried the brazier and the knife. As they walked along together Isaac said to him, Father. What is it, my son? he asked. Why, said he, we have the fire here and the wood; where is the lamb we need for a victim? My son, said Abraham, God will see to it that there is a lamb to be sacrificed. So they went on together (Gen. 22. 1–3).

We should notice the father's silence as he climbed the mountain of sacrifice. In the presence of his son Abraham could only keep silent, a silence hard to bear, and harder still as he came nearer to the place and the time when he must slay his own son. With the greatest care Abraham kept secret the order received from God which, while it struck him to the heart, gave him the power to go forward. He kept God's secret faithfully, and, obeying God, controlled the affection he felt for the son whom in a few minutes he must sacrifice. He could only do this provided that in the fullest degree he became a mere instrument of God, that this command of God had first made him sacri-

fice his father's heart, and had caused him, as God's servant, to shut his eyes to all that did not concern the divine
order, to shut his eyes to his own feelings as a father, and
the terrible consequences of his act. The very thought of
the consequences of the act which he was freely perform-
ing, and feeling so deeply, would have torn his father's
heart, and prevented him from taking another step. All
his energy had to be absorbed by this command of God,
if he was to accept it without discussion and with heroic
faith.

Isaac, the child of laughter and of promise, well beloved, was walking freely and joyfully beside his father,
all the time calling him father, as if nothing was happen-
ing, in utter ignorance. With a child's curiosity he ques-
tioned his father, and at once put the dreadful question,
the only question possible: "Father, where is the lamb we
need for a victim?" That was the great question, throughout the Old Testament, to which John the Baptist would
give the answer.

The instrument, carrying out, faithfully and promptly,
God's order, knew only too well where was the lamb. But
the father, whose torn heart was suddenly awakened by
this tender appeal, calling him father, could say nothing,
for he knew nothing else and could understand nothing
else than utter abandonment to God's mercy: "My son,
God will see to it that there is a lamb to be sacrificed." He
had not chosen the lamb for the sacrifice, but God himself
had.

So they went on together till they reached the place God
had shewn him. And here he built an altar, and set the
wood in order on it; then he bound his son Isaac and laid
him down there on the altar, above the pile of wood. And
he reached out, and took up the knife to slay his son. But
now, from heaven, an angel of the Lord called to him,
Abraham, Abraham. And when he answered, Here am I,
at thy command, the angel said, Do the lad no hurt, let

him alone. I know now that thou fearest God; for my sake thou wert ready to give up thy only son (Gen. 22. 9–12).

All was ready; everything prepared. Only at the very moment when Abraham began the movement to sacrifice his son, the angel of the Lord intervened, and called to him, "Do the lad no hurt." The ram outwardly took the place of the child, and was offered as a holocaust.

This sacrifice shows clearly that the outward slaying of the ram was of quite secondary importance. This was not what God valued most highly, but rather the intention with which it was done, the inner sacrifice, the worship of the heart. In essentials this was the sacrifice of Abraham, and not of Isaac. It was an inner testing, a testing of Abraham's fidelity, of the reality of his love for God. God carried this testing to its extreme limit in order that there might be shown more plainly the truly heroic quality of the servant's fidelity, of the friend of God, in spite of all the apparent contradictions in God's conduct towards him.

It is easy to grasp the entirely new character of this sacrifice, which no longer appealed only to the acquired or infused virtue of religion, like the two first types of offering, those of Abel and Noah, but demanded at once and explicitly the virtue of obedience, exercised in the light of a living and loving faith. The virtue of religion, taken in itself, consists in giving to God what is due to him. That is why it comes under the heading of justice, as a form of justice: it is justice towards God. Among the acquired moral virtues it is in one sense pre-eminent, because it is the virtue which draws us nearest to God. It is concerned immediately with his service, his worship and his praise. For this reason, apart from any others, it develops in a special way in man that which makes him God's image, that which binds him to God, and makes him capable of entering into relations with God. It is indeed the characteristic human virtue, in so far as man is a rational creature, entirely subject to the Creator and King of the universe. Upon our deep-seated, natural, desire for God it throws a certain light, derived from human reason, making this desire more consciously dependent, more thoroughly directed towards God, in his unique mystery.

The virtue of religion is like a higher virtue of politeness, which teaches us to live as creatures ought to live in relation to God, to conduct ourselves properly in his hidden presence, and in the presence of all that belongs to him. But this politeness is deep within us, a politeness of the soul, although it is expressed by certain actions. It is a politeness which is expressed by an entire devotion to God, a self-effacement in God's presence.

Together with grace and charity there is given us an infused virtue of religion, practised in the light of faith, and addressed in the first place to the loving majesty of the Father. The practice of this infused virtue of religion can receive a final development from the gift of piety. Breathed on by the gift of piety, worship becomes in the full sense a filial worship, the worship of the well-loved son.

Abraham obeyed God's command, and it was just in this act of obedience that he recognized the sovereign rights of God over him, that he worshipped that will which his human understanding could not fathom. Sacrifice, then, in the first place consists in the act of obedience to God's word. Abraham's act of obedience was concerned with the very person whom he loved most upon earth. It was not the first-born of his flock, nor the clean animals, which Abraham was commanded to slay, in order to declare the omnipotence of the Creator, but that very thing which made him a patriarch, and which he loved more than himself, all his hope and joy, his only son.

By this act of obedience God wished to remind Abraham plainly that the Creator has the right of life and death over all that exists, all that lives. He can require a father to sacrifice to him his son, and the father cannot, as a mere creature before God, claim the rights he holds from God; he can only be silent and obey. But God never acts in this way, simply by his sovereign authority, for it would be tyrannical, and God would no longer be acting as God and Father of his creatures. God requires this act of obedience from Abraham to test the fidelity of his servant and friend, still more of his friend than of his servant (the fidelity of the servant need not go so far as this, for the servant is faithful if he fulfils perfectly the task demanded of him). The friend is faithful if his heart is in closer and closer harmony with the heart of his friend, if his love for his friend is more and more a love deliberately chosen. If God wishes to test the fidelity of his friend, it is in order to reveal his own fidelity as a friend. The fidelity of God is such that, even though the external circumstances seem to contradict it, the contradictions are only in appearance, and behind these appearances his love is unalterable. It was in fact God who gave to Abraham his son Isaac, and if he caused Abraham to suffer this test, it was in order to give him Isaac the more completely.

That is why the act of obedience, required for the sacrifice, appealed directly to the patriarch's faith, hope and love of God. Such an act of obedience can only be practiced in virtue of a pure, unreasoning faith which does not doubt God's word, but is prepared to accept its divine meaning, and to disregard the apparent contradictions and absurdities. Abraham, father of believers, must believe in the fidelity of God, and of his promise, without wishing to justify it in his own eyes.

If Abraham had not at once submitted his obedience to the light of faith, if he had judged it by his own experience, his acquired prudence, he would have fallen into terrible distress, which would have almost paralysed him.

To carry out God's order he had to be willing to act under God's inspiration, without understanding. The prudence he possessed as a patriarch had to give up its most lawful rights, due in the highest degree to man, in face of God's demands, which only faith could answer. In order to become the patriarch of God's people, Abraham had to give up the use of his own experience in this great matter, so important to him, and to rely only on the wisdom of God. In order to enter into God's ways, and to act in accordance with them, he had to abandon all, to offer up all, and to sacrifice all.

By this act of obedience the patriarch was required to destroy his only ground for hope, both human and divine, the son who was the first fulfilment of God's promise and his only heir. His hope, in this act of obedience, had to go beyond that ground which was so lawful, to lose all support, and only rest on the merciful omnipotence of the Father. Abraham, in carrying out God's command, during those three days when he went up to the mountain, had to hope in God against all human hope: "Leave thy country behind thee, thy kinsfolk, and thy father's home, and come away into a land I will shew thee" (Gen. 12.1).

We have to leave all that is natural to us in order to obey this command of God, "come," an imperative order. Abraham, having listened to God with joy, listened to him with sorrow, for he had not only to leave his son, but to offer him in sacrifice, and there could be no longer a promised land for Abraham, since the sacrifice involved the destruction of him who was the true promised land. He had, then, to hope only in the almighty mercy of God.

We have already seen that, in God's plan, this trial aimed at purifying the fidelity in the heart of his friend. God required of Abraham, in this act of obedience, that he should love him more than his gifts, love him above the wonderful gift he had received in Isaac. The act of obedience expressed the choice of love, which God alone could demand. To choose God by sacrificing Isaac, sacrificing what the human heart of Abraham loved most, was truly to put God before everything and everybody. It was to witness that God alone is love, that God alone suffices.

In essentials this sacrifice was an act of worship, the fruit of the theological virtues of faith, hope and charity. Hence it came from the depths of his being. It was in the heart of the patriarch that his conversion to God essentially occurred. In the depths of his heart he distinguished in a new way between the divine and human. God required of him an exercise of faith so exacting that human prudence and reason were silenced; God required so sheer an act of hope that every human motive and support were left aside; God required so pure an act of love that all human love, however lawful, was as nothing.

Though the sacrifice demanded was not carried out externally, and at the last moment was completely altered, yet inwardly it was fully accomplished; Abraham had lived for three days with an extraordinary intensity, the presence of Isaac adding to it still more. To the inward sacrifice of fear, hope and love, there corresponded a new covenant between God and Abraham. God replied with a fresh generosity of love to his servant and friend who had been so faithful and so generous and who was willing to offer to him as a holocaust the only offspring of his race, by the promise of a wonderful fruitfulness, descendants without number: "I have taken an oath by my own name to reward thee for this act of thine, when thou wast ready to give up thy only son for my sake. More and more will I bless thee, more and more will I give increase to thy posterity, till they are countless as the stars in heaven, or the sand by the sea shore; thy children shall storm the gates of their enemies; all the races of the world shall find a blessing through thy posterity, for this readiness of thine to do my bidding" (Gen. 22. 16–18).

Indeed God had already promised to Abraham a great posterity: "And to that posterity I will grant increase, till it lies like dust on the ground, past all counting" (Gen. 13. 16). "Look up at the sky, and count, if thou canst, the stars in it; thy race, like them, shall be numberless" (Gen. 15. 5).

God had already made a covenant with him: "I am, and here is the covenant I make with thee, thou shalt be the father of a multitude of nations" (Gen. 17. 4). And he promised his everlasting covenant with Isaac (Gen. 17. 19). After the heroic act of obedience, God pledges himself: "I have taken an oath by my own name . . .", and God gives him an abundant blessing, which then becomes universal (catholic): "all the races of the world shall find a blessing through thy posterity" (Gen. 22. 16, 18).

This inward sacrifice, carried out through obedience, introduces us to a deeper contemplation of God's mystery. It is no longer only the omnipotence of the Creator, of the Father, which is experienced through the act of worship, it is in truth the fidelity of his love; God reveals himself as the Friend, in the strictest sense.

SACRIFICES UNDER THE LAW

The Pasch

The story of Isaac, Jacob and Joseph shows us in a remarkable way how God guides his friends, those whom he has chosen, with whom he has made a covenant, but from the point of view adopted here the story adds nothing to the great sacrifice we have just considered, for this dominates the whole of Genesis.[1] The Lord had said to

[1] If we wish to consider in detail the meetings of God with man, the dream of Jacob (Gen. 28. 10–19) must be specially mentioned, since it is the revelation of a special presence of God, just as the struggle of Jacob with the unknown, who did not tell his name (Gen. 32. 23–33), is the revelation of God in a kind of struggle

Abraham: "This thou must know, that thy race will live as strangers in a land not their own, reduced to slavery and ill-used for four hundred years" (Gen. 15. 13).

It was Moses whom the Lord chose to deliver his people from the yoke of the Egyptians. From his birth we find that God treated him with a special care. (Exod. 2. 1–10.) It was on the mountain of God, Horeb, that "the Lord revealed himself through a flame that rose up from the midst of a bush" (Exod. 3. 2). God called to him: "Moses, Moses; and when he answered, I am here, at thy command, he was told, Do not come nearer; rather take the shoes from thy feet, thou art standing on holy ground. . . . I am the God thy father worshipped, the God of Abraham, and Isaac, and Jacob. And Moses hid his face; he dared not look on the open sight of God" (Exod. 3, 4–6).

There will be no attempt here to analyse this wonderful meeting between God and Moses, when God revealed to Moses the loving and merciful care which he had for his people, and when God finally gave him the order to go to Pharaoh as his emissary to lead his people out of Egypt, when Moses, in face of this unexpected order, hung back and excused himself, trying to escape from a mission whch terrified him. Had he not withdrawn to the land of Madian to escape from Pharaoh who wished to destroy him? Now he must present himself before him. Moses thought more of himself and his own safety, than of that of his people. When Moses, having agreed, asked of him, who had declared himself the God of his fathers, his message, in order that he might be able to present himself to

between friends. Here it is not a question of acts of worship or of sacrifice, but rather of contemplation. The story of Joseph shows us the friendly cooperation of God with the man he has chosen to save his people from famine, after being rejected by his own family, hidden in the cistern and sold to the Egyptians (Gen. 34. 12–31).

Pharaoh with greater authority, then God, in answer to this demand, said of himself: "I am the God who is." Nevertheless, it is absolutely necessary for us to understand that this personal revelation of God to Moses directly commanded the sacrifice of the Pasch.

So Moses was sent by the Lord with this precise object: to get permission from Pharaoh for the people of Israel "to go out three days' march into the desert, and . . . offer sacrifice to the Lord, our God" (Exod. 3. 18). Since Pharaoh would not agree to obey the Lord willingly, God forced him with a strong hand by signs and portents, in order to frighten Pharaoh by showing him that his power was nothing compared to the power of the Lord. The last of these portents had a special character, having at the same time the object of preparing the people of Israel religiously, and also of punishing all the families of the Egyptians. For Israel it was the sacrifice of the Pasch, and it was the death of the first-born of the Egyptians. It was the passing over of God, who protected and saved his own people, and punished the pride and tyranny of Pharaoh.

In order to understand the true nature of the sacrifice of the Pasch, which was to play such an important part in the religious life of the people of Israel, and which was to be completed on the cross, we must always return to Exodus 12.

It was while they were still in the land of Egypt that the Lord said to Moses and Aaron, For you, this month is to lead in all the months, to be the first month of the year. Make this proclamation to the whole assembly of Israel: On the tenth day of this month, each family, each household, is to choose out a yearling for its own use. Or, if there are not enough of them to eat a whole lamb, the head of the family must call in some neighbour who lives close by, so that a lamb shall not be too much for their needs. It must be a male yearling lamb, or a male yearling kid, that you choose, with no blemish on it. These victims must be kept ready till the fourteenth day of the month, and on the evening of that day the whole people of Israel must immolate. They must take some of the blood, and sprinkle it on the doorway, jambs and lintel alike, of the house in which the lamb is being eaten. Their meat that night must be roasted over the fire, their bread unleavened; wild herbs must be all their seasoning. No part must be eaten raw, or boiled, it must be roasted over the fire; head, feet, and entrails, all must be consumed, so that nothing remains till next day; whatever is left over, you must put in the fire and burn it. And this is to be the manner of your eating it; your loins must be girt, your feet ready shod, and every man's staff in his hand. All must be done in haste. It is the night of the Pasch, the Lord's passing by; the night on which I will pass through the land of Egypt, and smite every first-born thing in the land of Egypt, men and beast alike; so I will give sentence on all the powers of Egypt, I, the Lord. The blood on the houses that shelter you will be your badge; at the sight of the blood I will pass you by, and there shall be no scourge of calamity for you when I smite the land of Egypt. You are to observe this day as a memorial of the past, a day when you keep holiday in the Lord's honour, generation after generation; a rite never to be abrogated. (Exod. 12. 1–14.)

All that the Lord commanded was carried out by the orders of Moses. This family meal was a religious meal; then was eaten "the victim that marked the Lord's passing-by, when he passed by the houses of the Israelites in Egypt, smiting only the Egyptians, and leaving our homes exempt" (Exod. 12. 27), as Moses declared to the elders.[2]

"It is a night," Scripture tells us, speaking of the carrying out of what had been proclaimed, "for keeping vigil in

[2] *Victima transitus domini est,* says the Vulgate, Moses adds when addressing the people and recalling the miraculous assistance of the Lord: "This custom is to endure like a mark branded on the hand, to be kept in view like a badge worn on the forehead; the law of the Lord shall be continually on thy lips; was it not the Lord's constraining power that rescued thee from Egypt?" (Exod. 13. 9). Cf. Numb. 9. 1–14, where the Pasch is presented as the offering to the Lord.

the Lord's honour, this night when he led them away out of the land of Egypt; the sons of Israel, age after age, must needs observe it" (Exod. 12. 42).[3]

Without pausing over all the details of the Pasch we may simply notice that we are in the presence of an entirely new sacrifice, which is presented to us as determined by the Lord.

By this new institution God wishes to take his people in hand, to give them a fresh sense of their religious calling. He wished, while granting them their freedom, to renew the will of their youth, as was plainly signified by the season when the Pasch was to be celebrated: "For you, this month is to lead on all the months, to be the first month of the year" (Exod. 12. 2; 12. 41; Numb. 9. 1). This sacrifice, this offering, was carried out at a religious meal, a family meal, among believers only, during the night, and in haste.

The Pasch implies a victim: "It must be a male yearling lamb, or a male yearling kid, that you choose, with no blemish on it" (Exod. 12. 5; Lev. 22. 19, fol.). Later the custom prevailed of sacrificing a lamb, which was slain, and the blood of which was a sign of protection by being sprinkled "on the doorway, jambs and lintels alike." The sacrifice of this victim was performed in honour of the Lord, to proclaim that he is the only true God, the God of Israel, and also to save the family of Israel from the sacrifice of the first-born.

Thus the Pasch shows the different judgements pronounced by the Lord on Egypt and Israel: to Egypt the passing by of God brought destruction, death and terror; to Israel it brought freedom and safety. The Pasch im-

---

[3] Cf. Exod. 12. 43–6, when the Lord gives Moses and Aaron further instruction as to the celebration of the Pasch: "No alien is to partake of it. . . . All of it must be eaten under the same roof; you must not take any of the victim's flesh elsewhere, or break it up into joints."

plies public worship, for by the celebration of this rite the Lord is recognized as the God who has saved his people, who alone can deliver his people from the yoke of Pharaoh.

This act of worship looks both to God's saving mercy and his avenging justice. It is under the influence of charity and of the gift of piety that worship can appeal to the saving mercy of God, of the Father who, full of pity for his children and wishing that they shall no longer suffer under the rule of a foreigner, takes them directly under his protection. Such an act of worship is performed with a certain homeliness of spirit, which yet reverences the sovereign majesty of him who said "I am the God who is," and who exercises his sovereign right of life and death over the whole people of Egypt, when they oppressed those whom he loved. Hence it is quite natural that such an act of worship should have been offered during a family meal, when all the members shared in the fatherly mercy shown that night, on the one hand in a spirit of homeliness, and on the other of a great solemnity.

For this reason, too, though the law had so many different liturgies for different sacrifices, yet the Pasch always remained the supreme sacrifice of the people of Israel, that religious people, consecrated to God. For this reason, again, when the temple, the house of God, was built, the principal sacrifice of the Mosaic law was not offered within the precincts of the temple, nor reserved to the Levites like other sacrifices, but continued to be offered at home by the father of the family. Hence it was that this sacrifice seemed to escape the legalism of the Law which to a great extent pervaded the whole liturgy of the temple. This sacrifice remained as the most spiritual element in the people of Israel, as its religious soul. We can understand why God began to train his people by means of this sacrifice. As I have said, it declared his almighty mercy, and involved the loving worship of a son who abandoned himself to the mercy of the Father. To take someone in hand, to train him, to teach him afresh, his complete confidence must be gained. But consider the difficulty of reviving confidence in a heart which has grown cold, generation after generation for four centuries. That is why God, in his wisdom, made use of a means profoundly, essentially, human, a family meal. He showed openly that all his power would be used in mercy to his people, that they might understand that this family meal could, by God's will, become a religious meal, a sacrifice which declared the mercy of God's majesty, and allowed them to participate in his saving mercy. Through this act of filial worship, this close communion with the mercy of the Lord, Israel gained confidence again in its God, and again found freedom.[4]

From that time Israel was to be able to serve its God in the desert, and to become a religious people, a people who belonged to the Lord alone, reserved for him. It is from this special point of view that we must understand the tables of the law, the commandments of God given on Mount Sinaï (Exod. 31. 18).

The laws were religious and fatherly:

> And now God spoke all these words which follow. I, the Lord, am thy God (he said); I, who rescued thee from the land of Egypt, where thou didst dwell in slavery. Thou shalt not defy me by making other gods thy own. Thou shalt not carve images, or fashion the likeness of anything in heaven above, or on the earth beneath, or in the waters under the earth, to bow down and worship it. I, thy God, the Lord Almighty, am jealous in my love; be my enemy,

[4] The Pasch was connected with the Sabbath, expressing an idea of liberation: every Sabbath, and especially the Pasch, should free the people of God from servile work. The Sabbatical year was also a year of rest and freedom. During this year special trust had to be placed in God, for this period of rest was for God's glory (Lev. 25. 10).

and thy children, to the third and fourth generation, for thy guilt shall make amends. . . . Remember to keep the sabbath day holy. (Exod. 20. 1–8.)

These commandments were intended to train a religious people, which should recognize that there is but one true God, worthy to be worshipped, a jealous God, who loved his people "jealously." The law showed the "jealousy" of God for his people. Plainly divine jealousy had not the same meaning as jealousy with us, which results from a too selfish love. God's jealousy expressed his overwhelming love for his people, the intensity of his mercy. He is a God who loves, and in this differs from idols and false gods.

The sacrifice of the Pasch, therefore, should be regarded as the means taken by God to allow the carrying out of his merciful will in regard to his people, as revealed to Moses on Horeb, and also as the foundation of the law, given on Mount Sinaï. The family sacrifice lay at the centre of the great revelations of God's mystery, and joined them together. The sacrifice was offered at night in the bosom of the family, while the other two revelations took place on the heights, in the brightness of the flame "that rose up from the midst of a bush," and on the mountain "wreathed in smoke, where the Lord had come down with fire about him" (Exod. 19. 18–19; 24. 16: "the glory of the Lord abode there on Sion, wrapping it in cloud").

The revelation of the fatherly mercy of God in regard to his people, the revelation of his hidden name, "the God who is," demanded from the people of Israel a fresh act of worship, allowing them to receive this mercy, to co-operate and participate in it. It was a loving, trustful, filial act of worship, which called for God's answer, the new covenant of Mount Sinaï:

If you live by my law, if you remember my commands and obey them, rain shall fall on you when fall it should; the land will yield its increase, and the trees will be bowed with fruit, threshing not done with by vintage time, or vintage by seed-time; you shall have food to your heart's content. Securely you shall hold your lands, sleep safe in your beds, with peace on all your frontiers. I will rid you, too, of ravenous beasts, and never the sword shall lay your country waste. You shall rout your enemies, and beat them down before you [. . . .] I will make my dwelling among you, and never shall my love cast you off, still coming and going in the midst of you, I, your God, and you my people. Was it not I, the Lord your God, that rescued you from your masters in Egypt, struck your chains from your necks, and gave you the upright carriage of free men. (Lev. 26. 3–7, 11–13. There is the opposite side of this covenant: "Will you defy my laws. . . . I will be quick to punish you with death" (26. 15–25).)

By means of the law of this covenant God revealed to Moses and his people his holy rights. He revealed to them his jealousy and wisdom as lawgiver.

Sacrifice of Elias

The liturgy of the various sacrifices was extended and more clearly laid down under the Law; it was a liturgy of burnt-offerings, in which all was burnt to declare God's sovereign rights, the supreme worship of sacrifice (Lev. 1. 1–17; Exod. 29. 38, 46), a liturgy of the offering of first fruits, to show God's rights over all fertility (Lev. 2. 1–16), a liturgy of welcome-offerings or peace-offerings, which showed that God alone gives peace, for he is beyond all strife (Lev. 3. 1–17), a liturgy of sacrifices for sin, begging mercy and forgiveness (Lev. 4. 5–13), a liturgy of sacrifices of expiation, to make amends (Lev. 4. 14–20). But the celebration of the Pasch (the feast of unleavened bread) always remained the centre of the whole Law—the supreme Sabbath with its seven days of rest.

These positive laws, which determined in detail the whole great liturgy of the people of Israel, codified in an explicit form what already existed in such abundance. It is unnecessary for our present purpose to pause over the different liturgies. They only interest us in so far as they show the particular purpose of different sacrifices: to worship the sovereign majesty of God, to implore his intervention, to recognize his absolute rights, to thank him for his blessings, to put things right so far as we can. All these public religious acts, derived from the virtue of religion, demanded an inner activity, a moral intention of worship, prayer, praise and contrition. Otherwise these liturgies would have been meaningless, and would have even become hypocritical.

They would have fallen into religious legalism, a dreadful and hateful thing, since in favour of what is external it neglects what is most inward, hidden in the depth of man's heart, that is, his personal relation to his God. Men supposed they worshipped God if they carried out a sacred rite of sacrifice, of burnt-offering, if they fulfilled the material provisions of the Law. We know how Israel, and mankind in general, has often slipped into his hateful fault. Then the precise, material practice of the Law kills its spirit.

Men supposed they had done their duty when they offered the sacrifices demanded by the law; the same attitude may be seen in the Christian today who thinks he has done his duty, if he has been to Sunday Mass, even though during the Mass he has made no inward act of worship or of love. It is thought that the inward attitude is of little importance, and that it is only necessary to give a material obedience to the commandment. What a hypocrite would the man be who deliberately acted thus! It is against this fault that the prophets declaimed with such energy, for such an attitude not only materializes worship, and utterly disfigures it by taking away all its nobility, but at a deeper level falsifies in man's spirit all true knowledge of God, regarding him as a kind of manager who notes material presence or absence, without troubling about anything else: it is recognized that God searches the reins and the heart, but it is forgotten that he is a faithful and merciful God, demanding above all a loving heart. The law was only a means for training God's people, and making them a religious people. Faced with this legalistic materialization of worship, this low appreciation of God's mystery, the prophets never ceased to recall that the Lord demanded above all a contrite heart, a loving heart, an inward worship, directed to God as a spirit.

> What do I care, the Lord says, how you multiply those victims of yours? I have had enough and to spare. Burnt-offerings of rams, and the fat of stall-fed beasts, and the blood of calves and lambs and goats are nothing to me. Think you it is a welcome sound, the tramp of your feet in my courts bringing worship such as yours? Vain offerings, bring them no more, this incense of yours is an abomination. Enough of new moons and sabbaths, of thronged assemblies where none but sinners meet! The new month begins, the feast day comes round, how it cloys the appetite! These be hateful tasks I can bear no longer. Hold out your hands as you will, you shall get no heed from me; add prayer to prayer, I will not listen; are not those hands stained with blood? Wash yourselves clean, spare me the sight of your busy wickedness, of your wrong-doing take farewell. (Isaias 1. 10–16.)
>
> Oh, but I am sick and tired of them, your solemn feasts; incense that goes up from your assemblies I can breathe no longer! Burnt sacrifice still? Bloodless offerings still? Nay, I will have none of them; fat be the victims you slay in welcome, I care not. O to be rid of the singing, the harp's music, that dins my ear! (Amos 5. 21–3.)

Appointed sacrifice they still offer, flesh of the sacrifice still eat, but the Lord will have none of it. (Osee 8. 13.)

A tender heart wins favour with me, not sacrifice; God's acknowledging, not victim's destroying. (Osee 6. 6.)

The prophets seem often to express regret for the time of the wandering in the desert; Israel then worshipped God with greater purity and sincerity of heart.

Though the prophets fought against this legalistic formalism of a law which was understood materially, and recalled the supreme importance of moral intention, of purity of heart and of understanding, we must not conclude that they opposed the Law, or neglected or wished to suppress the sacrifices which gave official, public witness to Israel's fidelity to its God. Worship of God had first to flow from the hearts of the faithful, from that which was most inward and spiritual in them, for it required an ever purer knowledge of God's mystery. To be entire and complete, however, it had to take possession of all their sensible and physical life, and become outward, and show itself. This was all the more necessary because the people of Israel lived amid peoples which worshipped false gods and idols. Israel was always tempted to imitate them, and accept some of their beliefs. For this reason God commanded them: "Do not ally yourselves, then, with those who dwell there; those faithless hearts will be set on their own gods, and when they do sacrifice to their idols, someone will bid thee come and feast upon the meat so offered" (Exod. 34. 15).

Moses and the prophets were to fight stubbornly against these temptations, and contaminations, which the Law condemned so plainly: "It is not for you to make yourselves gods of silver or gold" (Exod. 20. 23).

We must not forget that the first act of Moses, when he came down from Mount Sinaï, and caught sight of the golden calf, the idol made by the people of Israel, "a stiff-necked race," was to break at the foot of the mountain the tables of the Law which he carried, and which he had just received from God—those tables of stone on which the finger of God had written the ten commandments. This idolatrous people was no longer worthy to receive them, because it had already broken the first commandment on which all the others depended. In his holy anger, Moses "took the calf they had made and threw it on the fire, and beat it into dust; this dust he sprinkled over water, which he made the Israelites drink" (Exod. 32. 20).

The prophets never ceased to proclaim that the Lord was the true God and that the other gods were nothing, that idols had no power, and the chosen people were called to give faithful witness to the Lord.

Only two passages need be quoted; the first is from the prophet Osee:

> Spoke Ephraim, all Israel trembled at his word; how else came they, for Baal's worship, to barter away life itself? And they are busy yet over their sinning, melt down silver of theirs to fashion models of yonder images, craftsmen copying craftsmen's design! And of such models they say, The man who would do sacrifice has but to kiss these calves. Fades the memory of them, light as early mist or morning dew, light as chaff on the threshing floor, smoke from the chimney, when high blows the wind! [. . . .] And all the while I am the Lord thy God [. . .] from the land of Egypt; God shalt thou own no other, other deliverance is none. (Osee 13. 1–4.)

And Isaias:

> I call you to witness, the Lord says, you and this servant of mine, on whom my choice has fallen, will you not recognize the truth, and believe me? Will you not learn to understand that I am the God you seek? None ever came into being before me, or will after me. It is I, I, the Lord; no other can bring deliverance. (Isaias 43. 10–11.)

It is against this background of struggle to maintain in its purity the Lord's worship that we must see the unique sacrifice of the prophet Elias, in the reign of Achab, if we are to understand the fresh lesson it teaches.

At the request of Elias, Achab summoned all Israel to Mount Carmel, and the four hundred and fifty prophets of Baal and the four hundred prophets of the forest-shrines who sat at the table of Jezabel. Then Elias went before all the people, and said:

> Will you never cease to waver between two loyalties? If the Lord is God, then take his part; if Baal is God, then take his. [Faced with this clear choice the people made no answer. Elias went on:]
> Here am I, the only prophet of the Lord left, while Baal has four hundred and fifty. Bring us two bulls; let them choose which they will, cut it up into pieces, and set them upon fire-wood, without kindling it. I will prepare the other bull, and I too will set it on fire-wood still unkindled. Then call upon the names of your gods, and I will call on the name of the Lord I serve; and the God who sends fire in answer shall be acknowledged as God. (3 Kings 18. 21–4.)

The intention of Elias is clear. He appeals to the omnipotence of God, that God may show by a miracle that he alone is the true God. The situation is so tragic, hopeless from the human point of view, that Elias does not hesitate to appeal to this extraordinary means, which directly implicates God. The whole people approved what the prophet proposed. Were not the prophets of Baal, to whom Elias grants precedence, the more numerous? After choosing a bull and preparing it, they invoked the name of Baal:

> All day long they cried out on the name of Baal, Lord Baal, hear us; but never a sound came, and there was none to answer, dance as they would on the altar they had built there. When mid-day came, Elias fell to mocking them; 'Cry louder, he said, a God Baal is, past doubt, but it may be he is detained in talk, or lodging abroad, or on a journey; or he has fallen asleep, and needs awakening. Cry

louder they did, cutting themselves with knives and lancets, till they were all bathed in blood; but mid-day passed, and they were still prophesying; and now it was time for the evening sacrifice to be offered, but still no sound came; and there was none to answer them or listen to their supplications.

Then Elias bade the people come near; and when they were standing close to him, he began repairing the altar of the Lord, that was broken down. Twelve stones he took, one for each tribe that sprang from the sons of Jacob, to whom the divine voice gave the surname of Israel; and with these stones he built up the altar again, calling on the Lord's name as he did it. Then he made a trench round the altar, of some two furrows' breadth; piled the wood high, cut the bull into joints, and laid them on the wood. Now, he said, fill four buckets with water, and pour it over victim and wood alike. And again he bade them do it, and when they had finished, a third time. When they had poured it out a third time, the water was running all round the altar, and the trench he had dug for it was full.

The time was now come for offering the evening burnt-sacrifice; and as the prophet Elias went to the altar, thus he prayed, Lord God of Abraham, Isaac and Jacob, give proof this day that thou art the Lord God, and I am thy servant, and all I have done was done at thy command. Audience, Lord, give audience! Prove to all the people that thou art the Lord God, and art calling their hearts back to thee! With that, the divine fire fell, consuming victim and wood and stones and dust, and swallowing up the very water in the trench. At the sight, the whole people fell face to earth, and raised a cry, It is the Lord is God, it is the Lord is God! (3 Kings 18. 26–39.)

Among the sacrifices codified by the law, this sacrifice of Elias, appealing to the omnipotence of God for its fulfilment, seems entirely unique. It is an apologetic sacrifice in the strictest sense, a divine apologetic, God intervening miraculously to awaken a faith which was weak and asleep.

The miraculous fire which came down from heaven at the prayer of Elias not only showed the power of God's presence, his fatherly care, the absolute transcendence of the true God, who alone is worthy of worship and sacrifice, but also his overflowing love, his devouring presence, since he showed himself under the form of a devouring fire which not only consumed the victim prepared upon the wood, but took possession of everything, devouring even what should have quenched it, the water round the altar.

This sacrifice was offered on Mount Carmel, and not within the precincts of the temple, since it was offered in the course of a struggle, before all the prophets of Baal, Elias alone being a prophet of the Lord. This sacrifice, which was one of struggle and victory, appears all the greater from its simplicity of form. Only what is essential is retained, but this follows an opposite principle to that of other sacrifices. Ordinarily the sacrifice of burnt-offering expresses the inward act of worship. This act comes first, and gives the meaning to the outward acts, the sacrifice of the victim and its destruction. In this case the outward acts are first laid down as purely external acts, a fitting rite, involving no sacrifice. Elias would not have been right in telling the prophets of Baal to offer their idolatrous sacrifice, but he could tell them to perform outward acts, and await the judgement of God, signified by the descent of the fire, in order to bring about the inward act of worship. This sacrifice is wonderfully instructive. It shows emphatically that outward acts in themselves have no sacrificial power; they only perform a particular action. They are in the order of *doing* something. These outward acts are sacrifices only if they express and signify an inward act of worship, an act by which we acknowledge the sovereign majesty of God, our Creator and our Father, on whom we depend absolutely for all that we are. For this reason an act of worship of this kind can only be directed towards the one true God; to direct it towards a

"Baal," who does not exist, is to waste our time; it is to deceive ourselves and others, if the false act of worship is translated into outward acts of sacrifice.

The sacrifice of Elias shows, too, the close bonds which unite prayer of petition and worship. In some sense prayer here included sacrifice, as an attitude of soul far less determined than worship. Nevertheless, in its true character prayer means that we express to God all our desire, all our sorrows; it is the request of one who has nothing, of the poor man who reveals his needs to him who relieves them, who can help.[5]

Worship makes us nothing in the presence of God; we disappear as having no being before him who is.[6] Worship makes us nothing in the presence of God; prayer is an appeal, a cry to God, who can appear to us as at a great distance. Worship has far greater depth. It leaves everything to God. Prayer has a more subjective and affective character.[7]

It is by means of his prayer that Elias obtained his desire that the fire should come down on the victim; his prayer expressed the apostolic desire of his heart; he felt

[5] Expressions such as: "Listen to the cry of entreaty thy servant makes before thee this day! . . . thou wilt listen from thy dwelling place in heaven, and, listening wilt forgive" (3 Kings 8. 28, 30), are extremely significant; we find them in all the great prayers of Scripture, and in the promises.

[6] The following passage from the Book of Josue is very significant. Josue, when near Jericho, raised his eyes and saw a man who stood before him, with a drawn sword in his hand. Josue went towards him and said: "Art thou of our camp, or of the enemy's? Nay, said he, it is the captain of the Lord's army that has come to thy side. And with that, Josue cast himself down, face to ground; what message hast thou, my Lord, for thy servant? he asked. But first he was commanded to take the shoes off his feet, as one that stood on holy ground; so he did as he was bidden." (Jos. 5. 13–15.)

[7] It may be said that contemplation is a conversation between friends, when he whom God calls is present to his God; it is the struggle in a rivalry of love, and again the silent presence of love.

so strongly the lack of faith in the people of God, the extreme peril in which they stood. The fire from heaven caused an act of worship in all who were there. The sudden presence of God, shown symbolically by the fire, called forth at once an act of worship.

The sacrifice of Elias possessed a wonderful power from the very fact that it was God himself who replied, and intervened, and manifested his overwhelming love, by a miraculous fire. The sacrifice at once caused an act of worship; the whole people were seized with fear, and fell with their faces to the ground, acknowledging it is the Lord who is God. It converted the hearts of those present, declaring the truth of their faith in the Lord, the only true God, heightening their sense of the presence of the Almighty, and of the power of his jealousy: the fire consumed even the water.

This miraculous sacrifice is the great manifestation of the one, incomparable God, who watches jealously over his people and his prophets, who loves them as their friend, replying at once to their prayer.

Sacrifice of the seven brothers and of their mother

Finally, in quite a different context, and at a far later period, we should notice these last sacrifices, which yet possess remarkable features.[8]

The many martyrdoms mentioned in the Book of Machabees should be referred to, but we may regard as specially significant that of the seven brothers and of their mother in the reign of Antiochus Epiphanes, which was held in such honour by early Christian tradition.[9]

[8] The occasion was the struggle against the Seleucids to gain the religious and political freedom of the Jewish people. The chief hero of this story is Judas Machabaeus, whose father, Mattathias, had urged on the holy war against Antiochus Epiphanes, who profaned the temple and began the persecution.

[9] Churches were dedicated to them at Antioch, Rome, Lyons and Vienne.

These seven brothers and their mother one after the other chose to suffer torture and death rather than to break the law given to their fathers, each of them declaring with the utmost resolution: "We had rather die than break the divine law given to our fathers" (2 Mach. 7. 2); "Heaven's gift these be, and for God's law I make light account of them, well assured he will give them back to me" (2 Mach. 7. 11); "Man's sentence of death, what matters it, so there be hope in God, that shall raise up the dead" (2 Mach. 7. 14).

The youngest, whom Antiochus especially tried to win over, promising to be his friend and to grant him high office, if he agreed to abandon the traditions of his fathers (2 Mach. 7. 24), remained unmoved by such offers and persuasions: "What dallying is this? To the king's law I owe no allegiance; rule I live by is the law we had through Moses" (2 Mach. 7. 0).

Their mother, seeing her seven sons die in a single day, "was content to lose them all in one day, for the hope she had in God's mercy. What generosity of mind was this, that could temper her womanly feelings with a man's thoughts" (2 Mach. 7. 20–21). She reminded them of the sovereign rights of the Creator, especially over "the breath of life," and his almighty mercy, which should help them to despise themselves for the love of God's laws.

Her character shows itself more clearly in her attitude to her youngest son. The king wished to make use of her to tempt the boy by a promise to save his life.

Much ado he had to win her, but she agreed at last, counsel her son she would. And a fine trick she played on the bloodthirsty tyrant, leaning over her son and counselling him in her own native speech, to this effect: Nine months in the womb I bore thee, three years at the breast fed thee, reared thee to be what thou art; and now, my son, this boon grant me. Look round at heaven and earth and all they contain; bethink thee that all this, and mankind too,

God made out of nothing. Of this butcher have thou no fear; claim rightful share among thy brethren in yonder inheritance of death, so shall the divine mercy give me back all my sons at once [. . . .] And at length, when all her sons were gone, it was the mother's turn to die. (2 Mach. 7. 26–9, 41.)

By this martyrdom, which is sacrifice in the truest sense, these brothers and their mother not only gave witness to their living faith in the omnipotence of the Creator, who sees all things, and on whom all things depend but, at a deeper level, they declared their absolute trust, and their hope in the mercy of their God, who has compassion, and will raise them up to eternal life.

By their martyrdom, which was freely accepted, they acknowledged that their earthly life had meaning only in reference to eternal life. So too they witnessed that God alone is the source of life, and that for him death has no existence.

While the sacrifice of Elias acknowledged the truth of the one God, appealing directly to his omnipotence, here the witness is different, being given by "sons of God," who owe to a special assistance from the divine mercy their power to endure without failing the torments of a bloody death, and to remain faithful to the end to the laws of their fathers. The help granted them by God's omnipotence is here entirely within them. It is upon the hearts of these brothers and of their mother that the fire from heaven comes down, and brings about that heroic act of obedience, involving their death. Hence it is that the sacrifice includes in an act of obedience an act of inward worship, experienced in love—such an act of worship as allowed these brothers and their mother to regard their lives as nothing, to "despise" them, before the almighty mercy of their God and the exacting requirements of his Law. The outward martyrdom, the tortures and death, express the inward act by which they offered up their lives to their

God. They offered themselves freely to God, recognizing that he alone is God, that his law which expresses his will is holy, and that it must be observed even if this requires the sacrifice of their lives.

This inward act of worship has a special character of reparation. They are willing to offer their lives in order to make amends for the sins of the people of Israel, of whom they are members and with whom they acknowledge their close connection.

"Speed we amiss," said the sixth son to Antiochus, "it was our doing, that sinned against our God" (2 Mach. 7. 18). The youngest cried out: "Grievously if we suffer, grievously we have sinned. . . . As my brethren, so I for our country's laws both soul and body forfeit; my prayer is, God will early relent towards this nation, while thou dost learn, under the lash of his torments, that he alone is God. And may the divine anger, that has justly fallen on our race, with me and these others be laid to rest" (2 Mach. 7. 31, 37–8).

This act of worship, then, appealed in a quite special way to God's mercy, his saving mercy, having compassion on us and granting pardon, while at the same time it appealed to his justice, which punished them for their sins, and would punish Antiochus later on. This is emphasized by the brothers when, about to suffer, they said to Antiochus:

"Strange be his dealings with us, yet think not thee to defy God unpunished" (2 Mach. 7. 19). "Wait but a little, and good proof shalt thou have of his sovereign power, such torment thee and thine awaits" (2 Mach. 7. 17). "Archenemy of the Jewish race, thinkest thou to escape from God's hand?" (2 Mach. 7. 31). "And shalt not thou, by his sentence, pay the deserved penalty of thy pride?" (2 Mach. 7. 36).

This act of worship, inspired by great hope, was wholly

directed towards eternal life, and heavenly contemplation. It was a direct way of approach to the vision of God, and a strong appeal to the resurrection of the body. "Heaven's gift these be, he said, and for God's law I make light of them, well assured he will give them back to me" (2 Mach. 7. 11). The youngest expressed this great hope: "Brief pains, that under his warrant have seized my brethren of eternal life!" (2 Mach. 7. 36).

As a martyrdom this sacrifice possesses a unique reality and value, not merely as an inward act of living faith, nor merely as an act of obedience, like that of Abraham, but as the fulfilment of an act which required a gift of the whole self, consummated in death. This sacrifice is, therefore, "prefigurative" of the sacrifice of Christ on the cross, in a deeper sense than the sacrifices previously mentioned; in its reality it has a close relation to the martyrdom of Christ, which it foretells in a most striking and explicit way. It may be said to be the final preparation for Christ's sacrifice, and for this reason impresses us so strongly.

The martyrdom of the mother, who joined her seven sons, and cooperated in their sacrifice, in particular in that of the youngest, gives an extraordinary richness to this sacrifice. The mother assisted actively in the martyrdom of her sons, helping them as a mother should, comforting them, encouraging them "in her own native speech" (it is a mother who preserves the living language and traditions, and hands them on to her children). She herself died in silence. The prefiguration of Mary present at the foot of the cross, at Christ's martyrdom, of her "youngest son," whom she urges to be faithful to the example of the Elder son, of the elder sons, is remarkable.

This sacrifice, appealing to God's mercy, possesses a superabundance, a fullness of mercy. It gives access to the final covenant with God. And since it implies the gift of present life, surrendered to God in order to glorify him, God's answer can only be the gift of glory: "He who is ruler of the whole world, he, for whose laws we perish, will raise us up again, and to life everlasting" (2 Mach. 7. 9).

It is by the sacrifice of martyrs that the final promise of the covenant, the mystery of what lies beyond, is revealed to us explicitly and for the first time. Obedience to the Law led to the martyrdom. The Law, given to God's people as a divine means for their training, to make of them a religious people, consecrated to God, in the case of these seven brothers and their mother, attained its end in an ultimate and wonderfully efficacious fashion. The first commandment to worship God was carried out fully in this martyrdom.

These six great acts of sacrificial worship each have their own power, and hence reach a wonderful completeness, showing us progressively the mystery of the almighty mercy of the Lord, the mystery of the creative omnipotence of the Father, the mystery of unfathomable wisdom and fidelity.

These six acts of sacrificial worship demand on man's side the exercise of his religious activity, of his practice of theological faith, of obedience and penitence. They make man practise what is deepest and most personal in him, and deepest, too, in his whole social life, and social powers, and in his capacity to make use of all the fruits of the earth and of animals.

These six sacrifices, while perfect in themselves, yet remain prefigurations of Christ's act of sacrificial worship; it is from the sacrifice of Christ that they derive their whole value and meaning.

CHAPTER II

THE WORSHIP OF THE

SACRIFICE OF THE

CROSS

THE MYSTERY OF CHRIST CRUCIFIED

The sacrifice of the cross completes all the sacrifices of the Old Testament, giving them their purpose, and containing in a higher way all their perfections. This sacrifice is incomparably greater and more profound than those of the Old Testament; it is the supreme sacrifice, because it is that of the Man-God, of the Incarnate Word, who came into this world to carry it out. Nevertheless, to the Christian the sacrifices of the Old Testament should be ways of approach to the sacrifice of Christ, giving us an outline, as it were, imperfect but true and divine, of this supreme mystery.[1]

Like the sacrifice of the seven brothers and of their mother, Christ's sacrifice was also a martyrdom of the only Son and of his Mother. Jesus completed his earthly life with his torture and crucifixion in order to remain faithful to what the will of his Father required of him.

[1] Cf. 1 Cor. 10. 12: "When all this happened to them, it was a symbol.

The sacrifice of the cross was, too, an act of worship, making amends for the sins of the people of Israel. Jesus offered himself to the Father as bearing the responsibility for all sinful mankind, answering before the justice of the Father for the iniquity of the world. He is the Lamb of God, who bears the sins of the world. Christ's sacrifice is a pledge of eternal life. It opens heaven, and makes possible our entry into the Kingdom of God. It is inseparable from the mystery of the resurrection, of glory. Hence it is that to St John the mystery of the cross is the glorifying of the Father. Mary is silently present. She is given to the youngest of the apostles to help him remain faithful to the end.

Like the sacrifice of Elias the sacrifice of the cross, joined to the mystery of the resurrection, is the supreme sign of Christ's divinity, of the true divinity of him who sent him. It is the only sign Christ gave, a sign symbolized in the Old Testament by the prophet Jonas, who remained for three days in the belly of the whale. The sacrifice of the cross is a sacrifice that is carried out by the breath of love, the fire from heaven that comes down and consumes the whole victim. Jesus himself gave up his soul at the moment willed by the Father, when the Father (in his soul) took him to himself. When men nailed him to the wood of the cross, he showed by his sacrifice and resurrection that he had indeed been sent by the one God. The sacrifice of Christ on the hill of Cavalry was effected after a contest in which Jesus overcame Lucifer. He unmasked the kingdom of the Prince of this world.

Christ crucified is our Pasch, the true Pasch, the passing by of God who delivers us from the yoke of slavery to sin, and who leads us through the desert to the promised land, to the land of life, our heavenly home, to glory.

Before the cross came the Last Supper, and this continues for us in the mystery of the Eucharist, that divine,

family meal, by which we are fed on the flesh of the
Lamb who has been sacrificed.

The sacrifice of the cross is the offering of the true
Isaac, of the child of promise, sacrificed as son of promise, and as the scapegoat taken from the thicket. It is a sacrifice in the strict sense, carried out wholly in obedience to
the will of the Father, expressing the loving choice of
Jesus for his Father. Jesus knew that he crucified the heart
of his Mother when he accepted the mysterious will of his
Father; he knew that he crucified his beloved disciples,
that he drew them to himself, the Crucified One, to allow
them to be with him, and in him to be crucified. He was
prepared to drink the chalice which his Father willed
him to drink—"only as thy will is, not as mine is," he said
in his prayer to the Father in the agony of the Garden.

The sacrifice of the cross is the simplest and most perfect of the acts of sacrifice, or of offering, or of thanksgiving, purer than that of Abel, more perfect than the thanksgiving of Noah. By offering his body as a victim of love
and worship, he offered to the Father the first-fruits of all
humanity, the most excellent and wonderful thing pro-
duced by the world. He offered to the Father an utterly
pure victim.

The chief priests and Pharisees decided on his death
out of jealousy for one who was a brother but threatened
their religious predominance. Did he not blasphemously
claim to be the son of God? Had he not violated the law of
the Sabbath?

While the sacrifice of the cross gathered together in itself all the perfections of the sacrifices of the Old Testament which prefigured it, it was carried out too in a higher
way. What the types could not express—because they
were only types and, as such, could not proclaim what
types could not give—the mystery of Christ crucified carried out and gave us; it was the sacrifice of the well-

beloved Son of the Father, giving himself to us as our Saviour.

None of the perfections discovered and acknowledged in the types disappeared, but all were changed in this final consummation, the masterpiece of God's wisdom. The sacrifice of the cross is above all the sacrifice of love, the love of the Son for the Father, and of the Father for the Son, the love of the Father for us and of the Son for us, a love which is revealed to us and granted to us. It is the gift of the well-beloved Son, which was made to us on the cross. The mystery of the Eucharist bears witness to it, and communicates it to us, indeed to every man purchased by the blood of Christ. The cross is the great revelation of love for us, in that new worship in spirit and truth, accomplished by the Son. Or, if you like, it is a loving worship which wholly takes possession of Christ, and reveals to us his love for the Father and for us, and the love of the Father for him and for us.

These two aspects, worship in spirit and in truth, manifesting the mystery of love, are inseparable, but we have to distinguish them in order to explain them as clearly as possible.

THE MYSTERY OF THE CROSS: WORSHIP IN SPIRIT AND IN TRUTH

The mystery of the cross is essentially a sacrifice of filial worship, of reparation and satisfaction. St Paul tells us plainly: "Order your lives in charity, upon the model of that charity which Christ shewed to us, when he gave himself up on our behalf, a sacrifice breathing out fragrance as he offered it to God" (Ephes. 5. 1–2; cf. Ps. 40. 7; Gal. 2. 20). It is this supreme sacrifice which glorifies the Father, effecting an act of worship, the most profound, true, and filial that is possible.

Our Lord did not come to abolish the Law, but to fulfil it, to give it its final meaning and force. Since the whole Law, as we have seen, is rooted in the first commandment to worship God, and him only, it follows that Jesus, the supreme servant of the Lord, alone lived, in a special way, in accordance with the first commandment of the Law. He lived with such intensity of love that he transformed it, giving it a far deeper and more divine meaning —from the worship of the servant for his master was changed into the worship of the well-beloved Son for his Father. It is on the cross that is accomplished and shown in full all that filial worship which, throughout his life, Jesus never ceased to carry out and to be. The Epistle to the Hebrews states clearly: "As Christ comes into the world, he says, No sacrifice, no offering was thy demand; thou hast endowed me, instead, with a body. Thou hast not found any pleasure in burnt-sacrifices, in sacrifices for sin. See then, I said, I am coming to fulfil what is written of me, where the book lies unrolled; to do thy will, O my God." And the author of the Epistle to the Hebrews adds: "He must clear the ground first, so as to build up afterwards" (Heb. 10. 5–9; cf. Ps. 40. 7–9). The mystery of the cross, which is completed by the piercing with the lance, shows us this clearly.

To understand the change in the first commandment of the Law, to grasp the distinction between the worship of the Gospel and that of the Old Testament, we should consider the religious attitude of Christ, his prayer of worship to the Father throughout the Gospel and, above all, on the cross. We should observe, especially in the Gospels of St Luke and St John, that deep inclination in the soul of Jesus for the solitude of the desert and the mountain, in order to give himself up more fully to the prayer of worship (Luke 6. 12; 5. 10; 11. 1).

Undoubtedly Jesus had no need of solitude in order to

pray. He prayed to his Father always, but he wished to show us the need to leave all that is not God, to find him more perfectly, and pray to him more fervently.

Here I need only mention certain passages in which Jesus gives his teaching with special emphasis. When the Samaritan woman says to him: "Well, it was our fathers' way to worship on the mountain, although you tell us that the place where men ought to worship is in Jerusalem," Jesus teaches distinctly: "Believe me, woman, the time is coming when you will not go to this mountain, nor yet to Jerusalem, to worship the Father . . . ; but the time is coming, nay, has already come, when true worshippers will worship the Father in spirit and in truth; such men as these the Father claims for his worshippers. God is a spirit, and those who worship him must worship him in spirit and in truth" (John 4. 20–3).

The whole ritual of religious worship is always in danger of materializing what is purest and most delicate in man's heart, his appeal to God, his desire to worship him, by engrossing his attention with external details, physical actions and movements, to the detriment of what is essential, namely, inward attention, but this ritual is transcended by Jesus—not despised, but treated as quite secondary. The emphasis is on inward worship. Jesus accomplished what the prophets had already taught.

Inward worship is described as worship "in spirit." It is a worship which comes from the Spirit, which is carried out in the spirit of love, a worship which must spring from love, and take possession of all that is deepest in the soul.

It is a worship "in truth"; it must be directed to the one true God, and be carried out with an ever clearer and firmer faith, which distinguishes plainly between the mystery of God and all that is not God.

To grasp what this inwardness of worship implies we should compare the other passages in the Gospel in which our Lord demands from us inward prayer: "And when you pray, you are not to be like hypocrites, who love to stand praying in synagogues or at street-corners, to be a mark for men's eyes; believe me, they have their reward already. But when thou art praying, go into thy inner room and shut the door upon thyself and so pray to thy Father in secret; and then thy Father, who sees what is done in secret, will reward thee" (Matt. 6. 5–6).

"Moreover, when you are at prayer, do not use many phrases, like the heathens, who think to make themselves heard by their eloquence. You are not to be like them; your heavenly Father knows well what your needs are before you ask him. This, then, is to be your prayer. Our Father, who art in heaven, hallowed be thy name, thy kingdom come; thy will be done, on earth as it is in heaven" (Matt. 6. 7–10).

Yet we should not suppose that prayer, if it is good prayer, must be merely occasional. Jesus says the opposite: "And he told them a parable, shewing them that they ought to pray continually, and never be discouraged" (Luke 18. 1–6). We know, too, the parable of the friend who would take no refusal (Luke 11. 5). We must knock, and never cease knocking, until the door is opened, and this demands very great filial confidence. We can only pray inwardly, unceasingly, without giving up, if we possess an entire confidence under every trial (cf. Gen. 19. 17–35).

The confidence of a friend and a son cannot exist without genuine poverty of spirit and humility. Prayer, if it is to be effective, must flow from a humble and contrite heart, for otherwise it loses all meaning. To tell God of our merits and title to glory is not to pray, as we are shown in the parable of the Pharisee and the publican (Luke 18. 9–14).

What has been said of prayer is still truer of worship,

which should embody the more hidden and profound elements of prayer. It is this loving, filial worship which dwells in the heart of Jesus throughout the mystery of the cross. This mystery begins with the prayer of the agony, which is a prayer offered in private. Jesus was alone, without witnesses, for the apostles, even the most faithful, slept in spite of the advice of Jesus: "Pray that you may not enter into temptation" (Luke 22. 40). Jesus says to his Father: "Take away this chalice from before me; only as thy will is, not as mine is" (Luke 22. 42).

He tells his Father of the most natural and spontaneous desire of his heart and, while doing this, leaves the matter entirely to his good will. He offers him his desires, and leaves him to do as he wishes. Here is the inward sacrifice of the soul, beginning in a wholly hidden fashion. This offering is the loving worship of the Son, who presents himself to his Father, leaving himself wholly in his hands, telling him of his keenest desires, but at the same time offering them up to him. The loving and filial worship of the agony prostrates him utterly: "And now he was in agony, and prayed still more earnestly; his sweat fell to the ground like thick drops of blood" (Luke 22. 44).

This inward worship continued throughout the bloody sacrifice of the crucifixion; Christ worshipped his Father in the silence of his heart, worshipping in spirit and in truth. He worshipped him in the humility and extreme poverty of one who was an outcast, condemned by his co-religionists. But this worship in spirit and in truth was expressed with his whole nature, his whole body—worship in spirit and in truth does not mean angelic worship, exclusively spiritual, without any outward manifestation, but essentially what is inward, hidden, silent and loving. Just because it is a worship of love alone it needs to be real in a very high degree. It must be really carried out even in the body of the man who worships God; he must also be the victim sacrificed and offered up. While inward worship is expressed symbolically by means of an outward victim, an animal, a lamb, it always remains in the mind of the worshipper. In so far as worship is the fruit of love and entirely determined by love, the fact that it is in the order of thought and that its expression is symbolic opposes the reality of the love.

It cannot be content to remain in the order of thought and of signs, it strives to reach the thing loved directly for itself, and for this reason a true worship, fruit of love, cannot be contented with a symbolic expression. It seeks to become real in the most effective way. The filial, entirely loving, worship of his Father in the soul of Jesus was expressed in his own body offered as the victim of the sacrifice, and ultimately and supremely, in his heart. By his willingness to let his own body be scourged and crucified he was able to offer it to the Father as an act of sacrificial worship. His body was the most precious and excellent thing in the whole world, and thus he proclaimed officially the absolute rights of God over all humanity and the whole world.

The act of sacrificial worship is also a sacrifice to make amends for the sins of the human race. Christ on the cross made satisfaction for the sins of the human race. He was the Lamb of God, bearing all the sins of the world. He was the scapegoat, freely agreeing to accept the shame of all his people, of all mankind. He wished to appear before his Father as alone responsible for the sins of men— even for the sin of the traitor Judas. Christ offers to the Father his bloodstained body, all the wounds from his scourging, all the pains of his crucifixion, all the inward sadness of the agony in the Garden, in order to win forgiveness for our sins.

Hence it is that the sacrifice of the cross shows us the

wonderful mercy of Christ for us, while at the same time revealing the mystery of the justice and mercy of the Father.

All the actions of the apostolic life of Christ, the Good Shepherd, were plainly acts of mercy to his sheep, to all men. But it is in the agony in the Garden and on the cross that we really reach the mystery of his merciful heart.

All the sufferings of human sinners, all the consequences of sin, he made his own, accepting them freely. No suffering of mankind remained foreign to his heart; he knew them all and bore them all deep within his heart. Living with greater intensity than any other man, he bore them in his measureless love for each one of us. Suffering is proportionate to love, and hence it is so amazing that his mercy should be such as it is. He knew what he did. Being the good shepherd who knew his sheep with their weakness and needs, he knew that to be the good shepherd of men with all that this involved was to love the life of his sheep more than his own life, to be willing to put himself in the place of sinners, to be an outcast for the sake of his brethren, to be reduced to nothing, to be wretched, despised, and rejected beyond all others. The sacrifice of the cross, effected in the particular that it was effected, shows us this overflowing mercy. Nothing was withheld; he accepted all the sufferings, all the humiliations, the whole burden, and could go no further. Mercy consists not only in stretching out to help the weak, but also in bending down, like a mother, towards one who is fallen, in descending lower than him in order to succour him, in taking him up and giving him back his life. He was willing to be thought more wicked than Barabbas, a public sinner, a blasphemer, an enemy to the Law of Moses, who did not observe the Sabbath, a dangerous man who stirred up the people. He was willing to be a thing before which men veiled their faces, such that after death his body was not respected, his side was opened and his heart pierced.

Thus his mercy was a reality which affected his whole being, no part of his body remaining unharmed, and his soul experiencing the deadly sadness of the agony.

There is, therefore, in the sacrifice on the cross supreme worship and supreme mercy. In the heart of Jesus crucified, filial worship, far from preventing his heart from attending to his brethren, allowed him, desiring as he did to help them and comfort them, to be the true Saviour of his brethren, by bearing their sins and making amends for them and giving them a new life.

We are told this plainly in the Epistle to the Hebrews: "By a single offering he has completed his work, for all time, in those whom he sanctifies. And here the Holy Spirit adds his testimony. He has been saying, This is the covenant I will grant them, the Lord says, when that time comes; I will implant my laws in their hearts, engrave them in their innermost thoughts. And what follows? I will not remember their sins and their transgressions any more. When they are so remitted, there is no longer any room for a sin-offering" (Heb. 10. 14–18). The sacrifices of the Pasch, of Elias, of Abraham, and of Noe, are joined in a higher unity.

In the Gospel our Lord warned us that a legalistic and pharisaic attitude in religion could easily be very contrary of an attitude of mercy. We should remember the parable of the Good Samaritan (Luke 10. 29). Finding the man by the roadside, half dead, stripped and beaten by robbers, the priest and the Levite reveal themselves by their actions: seeing him they passed by on the other side.

We know from experience that it is easy to feel a certain conflict in the mind between these two extreme attitudes. It is easy to contrast the religious attitude with the merciful attitude. The religious man is separated from his fellows in order to be devoted to divine worship alone, to the praise of God. The merciful man, on the other hand, is wholly concerned with men's sufferings. The former is hidden by the majesty of God; worshipping him, he makes himself as nothing before God, and God alone absorbs his attention. The latter is lost amid his brethren who have been disinherited, and the more they are disinherited the more he desires to be with them, and the more they have a right to his help and his presence.

The merciful man only hears the voice of the poor, only the cries of the suffering, and the heart-rending appeals of the dying. This kind of psychological conflict could be described at greater length; we have all experienced it in some degree, and sometimes it becomes keenest among those men and those Christians who are the most generous.

Christ crucified carried out on the cross the most loving and most religious worship possible, and at the same time, as the Lamb of God, bearing the sins of the world, he accomplished the supreme act of mercy. In his heart worship and mercy were united in the fullness of charity.

Conflicts in the mind are indeed left entirely behind, absorbed by love. Christ's mercy on the cross consists above all in pardoning sinners, in making amends, in giving satisfaction, in their name. Now sin, in its most mysterious aspect, is an offence against the sovereign majesty of God. Hence in order to satisfy for sin the absolute rights of the sovereign majesty of God must be recognized, and this can be done fully only in an act of sacrificial worship in which the whole victim is offered, consumed, in order to declare the greatness of God.

Further, sin is above all pride, leading to disobedience, revolt against the law and the will of God. When the revolt fully develops and is all-embracing, it turns into a declaration of atheism. Then man, in order to be first, takes the place of God, calling himself his own master, depending on no one but himself. Instead of worshipping God and serving him, man worships man and serves him, denying God, killing him in heart and mind.

In order to make amends for this atheism and idolatry, which is the final stage of human pride, the Son of Man freely agreed, through love for men and in order to glorify the Father, to make himself as nothing in the depths of his heart and mind—the mystery of the agony—while this annihilation of self was expressed in the flesh and finally pierced his heart. To satisfy for the exaltation of the super-man, who desires his absolute independence, his entire freedom, the true King of men, the perfect man, wisest of all, the supreme man, had to accept responsibility for his brethren, and to choose the freedom of the Father before his own freedom, however lawful and natural.

Now the worship of the cross involves the complete annihilation of the human mind and heart of Christ through an act of obedience. Hence, just in so far as Christ on the cross worshipped his Father, and offered himself to him as a sacrifice in humble obedience, he could satisfy and make amends for all his brethren who were sinners. It was in order to satisfy and make amends for sinners that he lived through the worship of the agony and of the cross. What is true of the satisfaction made for the sins of men, as offences against the Father, is true of the mercy shown towards all the consequences of the sin.

Christ, the Good Shepherd, knows the sufferings of all men, and has made all of them his own, taking them into his own heart, as his own sufferings. He teaches us to make use of this as a means for greater love of the Father. Poverty, accepted as a punishment from God for our correction, can be a wonderful means to make us love him more, to make us live in more complete obedience to him. On the cross Jesus was the first to make use of these human sufferings; he accepted them in order to call down the Father's mercy more abundantly on all mankind and on all the Church. Jesus made use of these sufferings, which resulted from sin, as a means to beg his Father's help more urgently—does he not plead for us on the cross?— to lessen himself still more plainly and definitely, and to sacrifice himself still more perfectly. He sacrificed himself as the most wretched of men, deprived of all. He made himself nothing before the majesty of the Father, as the poorest, most despised, most humiliated of men.

In Christ crucified, the mercy of the Good Shepherd, anxious for the safety of his sheep, sympathizing to the full with their lot, and carrying the injured sheep upon his blood-stained shoulders, far from contradicting the religious attitude of worship which is wholly directed towards the majesty of the Father, is joined to it and makes it more intense. For he suffers with his sheep, communicating to them salvation and love of the Father, in order to let this love consume all and take hold of all. It is in order to associate truly his sheep with the act of worship and of sacrifice, it is in order that they may glorify the Father, that he shows such mercy to them. Christ's act of mercy is an act which does not stop at relieving the material sufferings of men, at getting rid of their punishment; it is not merely philanthropy, but a divine mercy, which rises up to God and to his love. For this reason the apparent contradictions between acts of religion and of mercy disappear and are transcended. Jesus comforts and helps his sheep, as the Good Shepherd, with a wonderful mercy and tenderness, in order to save them, and bring them into the presence of the Father, and that they may bring themselves into the Father's presence, together with himself and in himself, that they may unite themselves with his filial worship, his sacrificial offering. Mercy allows his act of worship to extend still further, and to reach the heart of every man, bringing them all to the narrow gate and to the Father's house.

We can say, too, that the loving worship of Christ crucified, his filial worship in spirit and truth, unites him so closely to the almighty mercy of God that it allows the heart of Jesus to be a living source of mercy. The more we are united to God, the more we can live like God, in conformity with his character. The higher we are raised in love of God, the more willing we are to go down deeply into our littleness in the spirit of love—these are the two aspects of worship: to rise to the majesty of God, and to acknowledge our nothingness—the more we can be filled with mercy towards all our neighbours, towards all who lack what they need, in every order of perfection.

We can even say that it is through the close union of filial worship and mercy that the sacrifice of Christ is above all the supreme sacrifice of love. The offering of Jesus on the cross, reaching its completion with the wound in his heart, is truly the filial sacrifice of love, the gift of his whole earthly life, to save mankind and glorify the Father.

"He gave himself up on our behalf, a sacrifice breathing out fragrance" (Ephes. 5. 2). He gave himself up in the freedom of love. He gave himself up to God for us, an offering and a victim; a sacrifice breathing out fragrance. It is in truth he who worships, who offers himself in sacrifice, who is given up for us. And this sacrifice is accepted by God, for it is a sacrifice of love which is carried out through obedience. The freedom of love with which Jesus offers himself is the inward freedom of the well-beloved children of the Father, a freedom which is not opposed to obedience, but is only carried out to the full through perfect submission to the Father's will. The more we are united to the Father's will, the freer we are, since we are then joined to our true end. It may be said, then, that the faithful, loving worship of Christ crucified is carried out through obedience, and this obedience allows this freedom for mercy and this abundant enjoyment of the merciful gift.

The sacrifice of the cross, together with the mystery of the resurrection, is the visible witness to the omnipotence of God's infinite love for Christ and his members. The sacrifice of Elias, before the priests of Baal, only prefigured it. The true fire from heaven is nothing else than the love of the Father which took possession of the soul and the will of Jesus, in order to let him act in a godlike way, to perform a filial, loving act of worship, the fruit of a moral virtue wholly transfigured by divine love, and performed in a godlike way under the breath of Love, of the Spirit.

If we wish to understand the divine unity in the sacrifice of Christ crucified, the unity of the mystery of filial worship and mercy, we must always return to this profound acion of the breath of Love which "renews the face of the earth," which renews the image of God in the soul of Jesus, and in his mind and will.

The breath of love which dwells in the soul of Jesus transforms all his actions, both religious and merciful, uniting them in love. Again, the breath of love, of the gift of piety, which turns worship into a personal act, makes the worship of the servant into a filial, loving worship. God, as Father, is then worshipped for his greatness, his majesty, as Father, as communicating life in its fullness. That is the reason why this filial worship is at first carried out in the depths of the soul of Jesus, in silence, in an utterly hidden and secret fashion. By means of the gift of piety love introduces into the soul its own character, its silence, its profound and secret way of acting. Love allows us to understand clearly that everything is related to the

one, supreme love, and that all which is not this substantial love of God is but "nothing."

The soul of Christ regards itself not only as "nothing,"
but also as at the service of all judging itself as truly responsible for all sinners, all sins against the Father. In
this lies the mystery of sadness which filled the soul of
Jesus, and left it in such terrible isolation, abandoned by
all. Through this weight of sadness and isolation the
action in Jesus' soul, which made him as nothing, was able
to reach its furthest point, that of desolation, contempt and
rejection. The filial worship in the soul of Jesus could
then experience the depths of poverty and nothingness.
He had to lose his soul in order to save it. That is indeed
the mystery of his becoming an outcast, and experiencing
this to the full.

In the filial worship of the agony and of the cross we
must look at the way in which the soul of Jesus made itself as nothing, an act willed and accepted by him, an act
accomplished in the total breaking of his human will—not
my will be done!—to leave all to the loving will of the
Father. This becoming nothing through love is joyful and
peaceful, but also violent and terrible; it bruises and
breaks the soul of Jesus, because the most noble, profound and delicate bonds of the human heart must be
broken and offered to his God, his Father. Jesus must not
only accept separation from his Mother, from John, and
from the disciples, in his condition on the cross, but he
must also wound the heart of his Mother and of his well-
beloved disciple. This violent "annihilation" of the will
makes the heart of Jesus a victim of love.

At first an inward act, love wishes for all. If the breath
of love, by and through the gift of piety, makes worship
an inward act, this very breath causes the act of worship
to extend to all the activities of the body and the heart of
Jesus. The whole of Christ's human nature is affected by

the breath of love, all is offered as a sacrifice of love, nothing is spared. God's love is jealous, and desires all without exception. Love cannot be contented with types, but desires the reality. The offering of animals ordered by the law had only the force of a type, and therefore was not enough: "No sacrifice, no offering was thy demand; thou hast endowed me, instead, with a body" (Heb. 10. 5). There must, then, be a reality which expresses the inward worship. The body of Christ and the heart of Jesus, as the blood-stained victim on the cross, expresses most fully this worship of reparation and satisfaction; the "annihilation" and inward love, all that is living in Jesus, must be consumed by the heavenly fire.

On Calvary the body of Christ himself is at the same time, temple, altar and victim, in the new liturgy. He is the Lamb and the scapegoat. He is the first-fruits of the world. Nothing can be fairer, or more noble or precious, than this holy tabernacle, this dwelling of God. All the riches and splendour of the temple are nothing in comparison with the worth and divine beauty of the body and blood of Jesus. His body is the most beautiful among the children of men, and it is also the body of the well-beloved Son of the Father, "who is the radiance of his Father's splendour" (Heb. 1. 3).

But the beauty of the body of Jesus is veiled during the great hour of Calvary. Only his weakness and defencelessness are apparent, and at a deeper level his sharing in all the dreadful consequences of sin is plainly seen. The scapegoat hides the lamb without blemish.

The breath of love, by and through the gift of piety, transforms the practice of the virtue of mercy in the heart of Jesus crucified. The divine practice of mercy is not content with relieving, helping, consoling, or paying the debt . . . mercy goes further. The place of the sufferer must be taken and, so far as possible, a substitution must be made, demanding a total gift of self. Jesus crucified gives all that he is. He gives his body as food and his blood as drink—a rich pasturage indeed.

St Augustine understood this well, when he said of Jesus crucified: "He ate with us that which fills the store-room of our misery; he drank the vinegar mixed with gall. That is what he found in our store-room. But at the same time he invited us to his splendid banquet, to the heavenly feast, to the table of angels, where he himself is the bread. Coming down on this earth he found every punishment in our store-room, and he has not refused to sit at our table to eat of them, while, in return, he has promised us his own table."

This divine mercy demands in return the gift of self on behalf of our unhappy neighbour, who can do nothing for us in return. We must give all we have, without thought of reward, an utterly free gift, absolutely unselfish. We must be willing to give to those who will make no use of our gift, or even a bad use. The mystery of the Eucharist shows us this mercy as freely given, unselfishly given, and given to all. Jesus gives himself to everyone, as though each was the only one to receive him, as though each was the only sheep for which, if necessary, the others would be abandoned, and yet he gives himself to all without exception. The mystery of the Eucharist helps us to understand the mystery of the mercy of the cross.

This divine mercy also grants pardon without limit, and especially claims the defence of those who have harmed us. Jesus on the cross pleaded with the Father for those who insulted and crucified him: "Father, forgive them; they do not know what it is they are doing."

This gift and pardon, which are granted only through the requirements of divine love let us understand how mercy, practised under the inspiration of God, far from contradicting filial worship, presupposes it and requires it.

We can only pardon those who have harmed us, if our heart is utterly filled with a friend's love for them. Because this love does in fact take complete hold of us, the injury does not influence us; we do all that we can for those we love. This is true even from the human standpoint, but can only be carried out fully as a result of the love of God, and above all as a result of the filial worship, which hides us and encompasses us, in the loving majesty of the Father.

Through love for the Father we are glad to pardon, to witness in our own eyes that his love alone matters for us, that his love is greater than these petty injuries.

In the same way the offering of self can only be carried out, if we no longer belong to ourselves, but belong to God. So long as we belong to ourselves, we cannot offer ourselves with the complete freedom of mercy. Our deep egoism prevents it. If we love God, if we give him the worship of a son, we no longer belong to ourselves, but belong wholly to him, and are wholly hidden in him. It is he who disposes of us according to his good pleasure. For this reason filial worship is necessary for the full gift of mercy, and of merciful pardon. He who no longer lives this filial worship cannot go far enough in the practice of mercy.

The making ourselves nothing involved in filial worship allows this fullness of giving, and joy in pardon. The mystery of the cross is a wonderful proof of this, and here perhaps we see it in its most divine and most human aspect. The Good Shepherd cannot be separated from the Lamb of God.

We can understand how the sacrifice of the cross, uniting in itself in a higher way all the perfection in the Old Testament sacrifices, is truly, in its essential nature, a sacrifice of love. It is truly the sacrifice of the new Law, which is the law of love. It is just for this reason that this sacrifice, an act of filial and loving worship, leads directly to a new revelation of God's mystery.

If we can start with the truth that every sacrifice of the Old Testament is a revelation to us of God's mystery, this applies still more truly to the sacrifice of Christ. For the Old Testament sacrifices only give an outline of the truth. They are stages in the revelation of the mysteries of God, who is formally distinct from these sacrifices, while the sacrifice of Christ lies at the end of Christ's apostolic life, at the end of his personal revelation, as summing up his whole apostolic life and teaching. On the cross Christ gives us his testament of love, and we must look for his final teaching in the mystery of the cross.

Our final understanding, therefore, of the mystery of God and of his attributes must be found in the mystery of Christ crucified. Hence, after trying to make clear the essential nature of this sacrifice, coming at the end of his life, we should try to grasp the way in which it unveils to us, in a final manner, the whole greatness of God's mystery: his love, his oneness, his mercy, his justice, his omnipotence and his closeness to us, his jealousy and his light, his charity and his holiness.

CHAPTER III

CHRIST CRUCIFIED: OUR WISDOM— THE REVELATION OF GOD'S MYSTERY

THE SACRIFICE OF THE CROSS: REVELATION OF THE MYSTERY OF THE LOVE OF THE FATHER, AND OF HIS ONENESS

When Pilate asked about his mission, Jesus replied: "What I was born for, what I came into the world for, is to bear witness of the truth." Pilate asked: "What is truth?" (John 18. 37–8). Jesus did not answer Pilate.

For our part we know that God is love, that all truth depends on this supreme truth, which is *the* truth. Hence all the Law and the prophets are summed up in this one commandment to love; if God is love, the Law must lead to love, and it follows still more plainly that the prophets must themselves lead to love.

The whole earthly life of Christ had as its purpose to give this witness: "What I was born for is to bear witness of the truth." It is by living to the fullest extent this mystery of divine love, as the beloved Son of the Father, that Jesus bears witness to the truth. All his actions teach us that we should love God, that we should understand his love, that we should love him as a well-loved Father. Jesus is the beloved Son, in whom the Father is well pleased, and he alone can reveal to us the mystery of the love of his beloved Father. From the crib, as a small, weak, silent child, he reveals to us this mystery of the oneness and love of the beloved Father. The first clear teaching mentioned in the Gospel tells us that he is wholly engaged in the affairs of his Father. Throughout his apostolic life he leads us towards the Father, and lets us gradually discover his love, but it is above all on the cross that he shows us, in the sacrifice offered for the glory of the Father and the salvation of his sheep, the infinite mystery of God's love. For this reason the cross is, above and beyond all, a work of filial love, and can be the most profound revelation of love. Love is not expressed, or certainly is always ill expressed, in words; it can only be expressed by love and through love. Now it is precisely the mysteries of the agony, of the crucifixion, and of the burial which are above all mysteries of the filial love of Jesus for his Father. Hence only these mysteries can reveal, by a kind of relationship which they bear to it, the secret of God's mystery, namely, his love. These mysteries are openings, which let us catch sight of the infinite love of the Father. It is through these mysteries that our Lord gives us his final teaching. These mysteries (the agony, crucifixion and burial), considered simply in the light of justice, and even of the virtue of religion, remain incomprehensible. Simply from the point of view of justice we cannot understand why such an extreme of sadness, pain and humiliation should have been permitted, when a single act of humility on the part of Jesus, having infinite value, could have made full satisfaction for all the sins of the world. From the point of view of the virtue of religion alone, the offering of the first-fruits of the earth would by itself have had infinite value, declaring the sovereign rights of the Creator of the universe.

If we consider these mysteries as giving the great evangelical revelation of the love of God, as the testament of the new covenant which is a covenant of love, then everything receives its full meaning. Nothing is out of place when it serves to glorify the love of the Father by declaring his exclusive rights as well-loved Father, when it serves to manifest the infinite greatness of God's love. Christ crucified has indeed become, by the power of God, our wisdom, our wisdom of love. It is foolishness to our little human reason—it was unnecessary to go to such lengths—a scandal to our human feelings. Being able to give in Jesus crucified a supreme witness to the mystery of God's love, wisdom has done everything to give this witness: death itself has contributed to this great epiphany of the mystery of God as Love.

If the whole of the Old Testament, from the standpoint of knowledge of God, is dominated by the revelation made to Moses on Mount Horeb, when God revealed his name: "I am the God who is"—the Lord, who is (Exod. 3. 14), the revelation of Christ crucified completes and perfects this revelation. Our Lord himself tells us plainly: "When you have lifted up the Son of Man [on the cross], you will recognize that it is myself you look for" (John 8. 28).

The words, "it is myself you look for," of Jesus crucified are those of the Son, declaring that "God is love" (1 John 4. 8, 16), and bearing witness to his love. In the silence of sadness and suffering he expresses all God's love. By means of this new burning bush, and in the flame of fire, the mystery of the Father's goodness is indeed revealed. We must try to understand the greatness of these two revelations, which put us in the presence of God and of his mystery.

When God revealed to Moses that he was the Lord: "I am the God who is," he did not do so of his own accord. It was Moses who wished to know his name in order to present himself to Pharaoh with more authority. Before this, of his own accord, God declared himself in a far simpler way: "I am the God thy fathers worshipped, the God of Abraham, and Isaac, and Jacob" (Exod. 3. 6).

To the exile, doubly exiled, God declared himself as the God of his tribe, of his fathers, as one in whom he could have absolute confidence, for he had made a covenant with Abraham, and the covenant continued to apply to all of his race. Moses, then, could rely on this covenant. By declaring himself in this way, God declared himself as the one true God, as the God on high, whom Jacob loved and worshipped, and to whom Abraham had been faithful. Moses, therefore, at once "hid his face; he dared not look on the open sight of God" (Exod. 3. 6).

By this act of making himself nothing, of worship, he showed that he too believed that the God of his fathers was the one God.

When Moses asked him his name, it was to reassure himself and to gain courage to confront Pharaoh, to bind himself to him in a more personal way, and to be able to use the authority of God himself. When a man presents himself in the name of someone else, he is clothed with his authority, and shares in his power. In calling himself the Lord: "I am the God who is," God unveiled the mystery of his absolute transcendence. This was necessary; he had to reveal himself as having authority over Pharaoh, for otherwise it would have been no help to Moses.

When God revealed himself as the God of Abraham and Isaac and Jacob, the heart of Moses was directly touched, for Moses believed in the promise, in the covenant made with his fathers. This revelation continued to concern only the people of Israel. To Pharaoh the God of Israel was the God of a people which was in exile, oppressed, and in slavery, the God of a despised race. Moses could not present himself to Pharaoh clothed with the authority of the God of his fathers. He knew what Pharaoh would think of this, having been brought up in his neighbourhood.

Revealing himself as "the God who is," the Lord, God revealed himself as the supreme Being, on whom all depends, and who has the right to give orders to Pharaoh. That the meaning of the revelation might be better understood, it was in fact accompanied by the grant to Moses of power to change his staff into a serpent, and again the serpent into a staff. "It turned to a staff in his hand. And the world came to him, Will they still doubt that the Lord God of their fathers, Abraham, Isaac and Jacob has appeared to thee?" (Exod. 4. 4–5).

Revealing himself as the "God who is," God revealed his name, that which expresses what he is, his own personality. The name of a person expresses what is most personal to him, what best characterizes him, and distinguishes him most plainly from other persons and other realities. To be told someone's name is to be able to call upon him, when we wish. It is to be able to attract his attention and converse with him. Thus it is to possess a certain claim upon him. God tells his name to Moses just in order to give him confidence and show him that he has not abandoned him, that he can go forward, and the Lord will always be with him. The name which expresses this mystery of God, which tells us what is unique in God, is an ineffable name, the Lord, a name which cannot be named, meaning "is": in this way it is that God declares himself to Moses, when he asks his name: "I am the God who is." God uses the verb "to be" to express what he is; he uses the verb which has the most common and general meaning. Certainly the verb "to be" is present in all our assertions, whether implicitly or explicitly. It has also the most basic and profound meaning, for, if a reality is not, we can make no assertion about it. Since it has the deepest meaning of all, no one else can give as his name "I am who is," that is, "I am he who is before all, at the source of all." Hence, in calling himself the Lord, God both hides and reveals himself.[1] He makes clear to Moses that he cannot be defined, for a definition cannot be given by using a verb which is, the basis of all our assertions. To give himself such a name as this is to disavow any particular characteristic, and so any possibility of definition. God cannot be defined for, in order to define God, we should have to reach something beyond being. Calling himself the Lord, he also reveals himself in a wonderful way. He reveals the absolute simplicity of his being, since he has no other determination, no other characteristic, but to be. In giving as his name, "I am," he reveals to us that he is before all that exists in a particular manner. He himself exists in an absolute manner, while all other realities exist only in a partial, particular manner.

Thus he also contrasts himself with other gods, who are but nothing. He contrasts himself with the gods of Pharaoh who are nothing and can do nothing. Even though Pharaoh did not acknowledge the Lord as the one true God, this does not affect the fact that "he is." This revelation, made in germ to Moses, will become more explicit in the prophets, and assume outstanding importance.

[1] Cf. *Bible de Jérusalem,* éd. du Cerf, 1956, p. 63—with reference to the two interpretations of the name of the Lord—one, emphasizing the negative aspect: God declares, "I am who I am," the other, emphasizing the positive aspect: "I am he who is." In general, tradition has preferred the second.

Here I will only quote some passages from the prophet
Isaias.

> I am the Lord, whose name tells of power; I will not let
> the boast that is mine pass to another, or share my renown
> with graven gods. [42. 8.] None ever came into being be-
> fore me, or will after me. It is I, I, the Lord; no other can
> bring deliverance. [. . .] I am God, and what I was, I am;
> from my power there is no escaping; when I execute my
> designs, none can avert them. [43. 10, 13.] I am before all;
> there is no other God but I. What other is like me. [44. 6.]
> It is the Lord that speaks, and there is no other to rival me,
> no God but I; I, still unknown to thee, was fain to make
> thee strong, to what end? Because I would proclaim it from
> east to west that there is no other God. [45. 5–6; cf. 18.
> 20–2; 46. 5–7; 48. 11.] It is the Lord that speaks, and
> there is no other to rival me; I, the fashioner of darkness,
> the creator of light, I, the maker of peace, the author of
> calamity. I, the Lord, am the doer of all this. [45. 6–7.]
> Truly, God of Israel, our Saviour, thou art a God of hidden
> ways! All the makers of false gods must needs be dis-
> appointed, must go away ashamed and abashed. [45. 15–16.]

Revealing himself as the Lord, "I am the God who is,"
he reveals himself as the Master of all because he is before all, and all things depend on him. For that reason he
has no rival, for nothing is equal to him. He has no relation to anything, but all is relative to him, and so his name
can only be "the God who is." No other name can be so
simple, or better express the absolute simplicity of the
source of all, or better express the transcendence of the
Creator of the universe.

The revelation on Mount Horeb remains true for ever:
he who gave us his name that we might be able to call
upon him, is always the same Lord. It is our part to receive this revelation with faith, and to live in accordance
with it. On the cross, however, the Lord revealed himself
to us in a new way: "he who is" is the Saviour who gives
himself to us through love. Jesus' sacrifice on the cross is
the new burning bush, which reveals that God, in all his

being, in all the purity and simplicity of his being, is love. If God were not love in all his being, in all that he is, the sacrifice of Jesus on the cross, of him who said "I am," could have no meaning, would be foolishness and a scandal. If God is love this sacrifice is indeed wisdom, the great manifestation of love.

The new sign, given us that we may understand that God is love in all his being, that "I am" is love, is the resurrection of the body of Jesus, the resurrection of the Lamb, the glorification of his wounded heart—the wood of life becomes a serpent (loaded with all the iniquity of the world, he is the cursed and abandoned one), and the serpent, the cursed one, becomes again the wood of life.

The "hand of God," on the cross and in the agony, is covered with leprosy, white as snow, being plunged in the Father's will, and again it is seen to be pure, being hidden in the will of the Father, in his love.[2]

The bloody sacrifice of Jesus reveals to us above all how absolute is the love of God. God is love; his love is as simple as his being. In us love is always relative; always shared in; it is not at its source. We cannot be love in all our being. There is in the depths of our being a certain metaphysical egoism, which limits our love at the root. We can only love in successive acts which remain, whatever their intensity and vehemence, always accidental, that is, always an addition to our substantial being. This cleavage in every creature between its substantial being and its love, whether passionate or spiritual, shows how radically limited are our hearts, which cannot set on fire our whole being, and when it seems to us to burn, this

[2] This is the second sign given to Moses: "Put thy hand into thy bosom; and, doing so, he found that it came out a leper's hand, white as snow. And now the Lord had a fresh command for him, Put it back in thy bosom again; so he put it back, and this time, when he brought it out, the skin on it was no different from the rest of his skin" (Exod. 4. 6–7).

is only a passing impression; in reality it is not all on fire; there is always something which cannot burn, which cannot change into fire, that is, into love. On the other hand all God's being is love, for he is love. Even the Old Testament declared the love of God.

The use of the symbol of fire, to express the active presence of God, is very clear (cf. Gen. 15. 17, the covenant with Abraham; Exod. 13. 21, the pillar of fire, leading Israel across the desert; Exod. 19. 18, Sinaï on fire). The very name of the Lord was revealed to Moses from the burning bush. The angel of the Lord manifested himself to him (Moses) under the form of a flame of fire bursting from a bush: "it seemed that the bush was alight, yet did not burn" (Exod. 3. 2); "The whole of Mount Sinaï was by now wreathed in smoke, when the Lord had come down with fire about him" (Exod. 19. 18); on Mount Carmel we are told: "the divine fire fell, consuming victim and wood" (3 Kings 18. 38). But we are also told that the Lord was not this "fire," that he was in the fire (3 Kings 19. 12).

Apart from the symbolism of fire we are told expressly that God loved his people, and hence that he is love. It is especially with the prophets that we find the deeper revelations of the Lord's heart:

"Out there in the solitude they have won pardon, those exiles the sword left untouched; Israel shall find a home, the Lord says, the Lord, making himself known from far away. With unchanging love I love thee, and now in mercy I have drawn thee to myself" (Jer. 31. 2–3, cf. Deut. 4. 37; 10. 15; Isaias 43. 4). "Forget not, Lord, thy pity, the mercies of long ago" (Ps. 24. 6).

In the prophet Osee the revelation of God's love is still clearer:

"Israel in his boyhood, what love I bore him! Away from Egypt I beckoned him, henceforth my son. . . . Yet it was I, none other, guided those first steps of theirs, and took them in my arms, and healed, all unobserved, their injuries. Sons of Adam, they should be drawn with leading-strings of love; never waggoner was at more pains to ease bridle on jaw, feed beast so carefully" (Osee 11. 1–4).

After the exile the Lord again declared his love for Israel:

> Not thine to fear disappointment, not thine to blush for hope unfulfilled. [. . .] Husband now thou hast, and the name of him is the Lord of hosts, thy creator; he, the Holy One of Israel, that now will be called God of the whole earth, makes thee his own. The Lord calls thee back, a woman forsaken and forlorn, the wife of his youth, long cast away; thy God sends thee word, If I abandoned thee, it was but for a little moment, and now, in my great compassion, I bring thee home again. Hid I my face from thee, it was for a short while, till my anger should be spent; love that takes pity on thee shall be eternal, says the Lord, thy ransomer. (Isaias 54. 4–8.)

We should also remember the Canticle of Canticles, which expresses clearly this power of love and its primacy. To show the nature of this love the Lord says with emphasis: "The very name of the Lord bespeaks jealous love, he will endure no rival" (Exod. 34. 14). He allows no sharing in this love.

The mystery of the Incarnation manifests to us the mystery of the love of God, which is exercised through the gift he gives, and through the gift of a person. By giving us his Son, and by giving him in the way in which he has chosen to give him, he makes us understand how he loves us, and thus we discover the sweetness and power of his love: "What has revealed the love of God, where we are concerned, is that he has sent his only-begotten Son into the world, so that we might have life through him. That love resides, not in our shewing any love for

God, but in his shewing love for us first, when he sent out his Son to be an atonement for our sins" (1 John 4. 9–10; cf. John 3. 16).

The sacrifice of the cross reveals to us with fresh force the "jealousy" of his love, its absolute quality, and at a still deeper level how his love is ultimate and substantial. The death of Christ, freely accepted, which witnesses to the love of the Father, is stronger than death, the victor over every death. Death alone can be a sign of the absolute and substantial primacy of God's love.

Every word, every human action, other than death, can be corrected, repaired, finished and perfected, for all these actions are essentially relative, while death alone affects us in a way which is total and final, and it cannot be corrected, or perfected. Death alone is without remedy, for it is a substantial separation. Alone in our world of sense it imposes itself in an absolute fashion. It is the only absolute, which can be palpable in any sense to us, at once terrible and fascinating. Our senses tremble at it, for they do not love it, but regard it as an enemy. Our senses are only at ease with relativity and movement, but at the same time our understanding, in its purest, most spiritual, and most immaterial element, is drawn, we may almost say, towards death, or, to be more accurate, can be lead on by it, on account of the thirst both for experience or for the ultimate. Now death presents itself to us at once as a still untried experience, and as an ultimate, negative it is true, but still ultimate and absolute.

We see, then, that, through the fact that it is perceived by the senses, and has an absolute value as the end, death can be used by God's wisdom as the sign which is best able to express clearly the greatness of his love, which is substantial, eternal, and incomparable.

In this life, with its narrow wisdom of love, man judges instinctively, when he loves, that death alone can express the intensity of his love. Do not lovers claim that their love is stronger than death? If they could, would they not make use of death to prove their love?

What human love only stirs up as an abstract desire, since human love depends on our state in the present life, and would destroy itself by death, this God's love can accomplish, for such love is in truth stronger than death. It rules over it, and can make use of it to proclaim its own absolute character and supremacy.

Christ's death on the cross, freely accepted through love, witnesses plainly to the supremacy of God's love, of the love of the Father.

Since God's wisdom uses the death of the Man-God on Calvary to manifest the substantial character of God's love, it is fitting that it should use it to the full. Hence it is that all the deaths man can suffer are, so to speak, gathered together in this one death. In the death of Christ they all, in their various degrees, possess an extreme intensity, in order to assert the more emphatically that God's love alone is substantial love, pure love.

Let us think of the death, unperceived and solitary, of the agony in the Garden—"My soul is ready to die with sorrow" (Mark 14. 34), said Jesus. Agony and terror dismay and oppress him. This was the inward death of the soul, which today we should call the death of the psychological Ego, of the psychological personality. Jesus utterly gives up his whole human will before the will of the Father—"not my will but thine be done!" This was a hidden, and infinitely mysterious death, in which Jesus suppresses himself, and is willing to be as it were forsaken: death in sadness, agony and strife.

Then there comes the kiss of Judas, the sign of betrayal, the cowardice of the disciples who, seeing Jesus seized, fled away, the denial of Peter, in whom Jesus had placed such trust. Betrayal, cowardice, denial, in these different ways the heart of a friend can die. Betrayal of a friend is indeed death to friendship in the strictest sense, and here death is accompanied by cowardice and denial, that it may be complete in its intensity and in its effects. One alone remains faithful. This is truly a death which the human heart suffers, if we realize that friendship is one of the deepest ways in which the human heart can express itself.

All the humiliations of the Pretorium, when he was scorned and derided by the soldiers who thought him a mere madman, when the Chief Priests regarded him as a blasphemer, who did not respect God's rights, when he was considered a dangerous adventurer, who might seduce the people, when the life of the criminal, Barabbas, was chosen before his life, and when he was condemned to the most degrading of punishments, the punishment of slaves—he experienced every humiliation, and through these humiliations he experienced every degradation, political and religious. He died to the life of a free citizen, a member of a political society. He died to the life of a religious man, a member of a religious society—these are truly deaths, for there is a real human development on both these levels.

Then, the crucifixion meant physical death, the violent and bloody death of the cross, led up to by the scourging and the crowning with thorns, that this death might be still more cruel and shameful. This form of death is the most painful and violent possible.

Even his corpse was not respected: "When they came to Jesus, and found him already dead, they did not break his legs, but one of the soldiers opened his side with a spear" (John 19. 33–4). It was necessary that his breast should be opened, and his heart pierced, that the last drop of his blood might be shed. This final death of his corpse was necessary; Jesus, being dead, could speak no longer, but his heart could still bleed.

Each of these deaths, together with the different man-

ners of his resurrection which are implied, bear witness
that the love of God is the only eternal, substantial love.
It is the only faithful love, the only love which is the
source of life. And all these deaths were completed
through the wounding of the heart of Jesus. This open
wound in the heart of Jesus is, as it were, a divine opening which lays bare the abyss of God's love, which gives
it to us and reveals it, which expresses it as a reality for us.

Through his wounded side, through his martyr's heart,
we can enter as by a royal door, narrow indeed, in order
to contemplate the mystery of the filial love, by which the
Son is wholly delivered to the Father's good pleasure, who
truly loves his beloved Son. "This my Father loves in me,
that I am laying down my life, to take it up again afterwards. Nobody can rob me of it; I lay it down of my own
accord. I am free to lay it down, free to take it up again;
that is the charge which my Father has given me. . . .
And he who sent me is with me; he has not left me all
alone, since what I do is always what pleases him" (John
10. 17–18; 8. 29).

In this love of the Son is revealed to us the love of the
Father for the beloved Son, the mystery of the love of
God, as it had never yet been revealed. This is truly the
jealous God, and his love which excludes all else, his substantial, inward love, which is revealed to us and given us.

When we reach the love of God, we reach what is
deepest, most inward, most personal in God, if this mode
of expression may be used. It is indeed, as it were, the
"heart" of God which is revealed to us in the heart of
Jesus crucified, in and through the wounded heart of
Christ, in order to make us understand that, if God, in
the simplicity of his being, cannot be reached by any
creature—he is one whom we cannot affect, but who acts
on us—God, in the fullness of his love, is the most vulner-
able of beings, the being in whom there is no hardness, or

egoism, or bitter, cold, indifferent return into himself, for he is love. It is truly love which makes us attentive to others, receptive, able to experience the feelings of others, to live what they live. God, in his whole personality, is love. Hence, in his whole personality, he is receptive. He is one who draws us to himself, and wishes to hide us in the very mystery of his love.

If the covenant of the first Pasch was made in the light and the mystery of the simplicity of him who said: "I am the God who is," the covenant of the true, final Pasch, which frees us from the slavery of sin, is made in the light of the mystery of love, of him who in silence gives to us as a sign of supreme love the wounded heart of his beloved Son.

We should understand that this revelation of God's love, far from contradicting the revelation of his simplicity of being, gives it, on the contrary, its profound meaning, for in God simplicity of being and love are but one. The love of God is simple and pure; God is the purity of love. The simplicity of God's being is love; it is no mere abstract simplicity, but the simplicity of one who is perfect in love, with a clear, burning simplicity. It is the very simplicity of love. Scripture makes use of the symbol of a column to make us understand this simplicity of love, to express its freshness and richness. God always loves as though it were the first act of love, and he always loves as though it were the final act of love.

Horeb and the cross are indeed inseparable; the two Paschs are inseparable.

THE SACRIFICE OF THE CROSS: THE REVELATION OF THE MYSTERY OF THE JUSTICE AND MERCY OF THE FATHER

The sacrifice of the cross reveals to us the mystery of the substantial love of God, but it also reveals to us, in a

new way, his mercy and justice. It reveals to us especially
the close harmony in God between these two divine
attributes already revealed so emphatically in the Old
Testament, which may sometimes appear contradictory.

First we shall see how the sacrifice of the cross gives
the revelation of justice and mercy and then how, by giving this revelation, it leads up to their divine harmony.

The revelation of God's justice begins in the first pages
of Scripture. After the sin of Adam and Eve we see how
God judges Adam and Eve and the serpent, awarding
each a punishment in proportion to their sin (Gen. 3.
14–19). There is an act of judging and an act of justice,
for God is both the person offended, as law-giver, and the
judge. So too with Cain, when he killed Abel, we see God
judging by punishing the slayer of his brother (Gen. 4.
10–16). Again, the flood is an act of justice on the part of
the Lord (Gen. 5. 7), as also is the scattering of those who
wished to build the tower of Babel (Gen. 11. 8).

At the end of the revelation, in the Apocalypse, the
justice of God still appears to have great importance in
God's government.

Throughout the whole of Scripture this mystery of
God's justice is stated clearly. At the same time, however,
something still more mysterious has been revealed to us:
certain acts of pardon, of protection, of care, of pity: although God is just he appears as merciful.

Before the sin of Adam it is God's care of him, freely
bestowed, which is revealed to us, when he says: "It is
not well that man should be without companionship"
(Gen. 2. 18). In the cases of Abel and Noah the merciful
goodness of God is revealed: "On Abel, and on his offering, the Lord looked with favour" (Gen. 4. 4). "Only on
Noah did God look with favour" (Gen. 6, 8), and especially the covenant which the Lord made with Noah:
"Never again will I plague the earth on man's account,

that has all the thoughts and imaginations of his heart, even in youth, so bent towards evil" (Gen. 8. 21).

But it is especially in regard to the patriarchs, and perhaps still more in regard to Moses, that the mercy of the Lord is manifested fully. Appearing to Moses, he says: "I have not been blind to the oppression which my people endure in Egypt, I have listened to their complaint about the cruelty of the men who are in charge of their work. I know what their sufferings are, and I have come down to rescue them from the power of the Egyptians; to take them away into a fruitful land and large, a land that is all milk and honey" (Exod. 3. 7–8).

This is a wonderful description of the merciful God; he has seen the misery of his people. The first requirement of mercy is to know the unhappiness of the other person; it is necessary to pay special attention, to find out the misery, and to be able to look at it squarely. Yet it must be looked at with a friend's look, otherwise it will cause fear. To look at the misery merely for the sake of looking at it, to use it as an experiment, is surely inhuman. What should we think of a doctor who took away the dressing from a patient and thereby did him harm, merely to see how the wound was? God has seen the misery of his people.

The second requirement of mercy is sympathy with the other person's misery, to know it as though it were our own. Everything must be done to comfort the unhappy: "I have come down to rescue them from the power of the Egyptians." God wished to make use of Moses in order to carry out this great act of mercy towards his people. And this is the way in which God showed his mercy: he wished to do so with a special delicacy, to save his people by means of a member of his people. This was due to God's merciful character, for God did not need Moses in order to carry out his will, but he wished to make use of him, in order that his act of mercy might be the more perfect, the more fitting for the unhappy people he wished to deliver. In face of the objections and hesitations of Moses, who was afraid to carry out such a mission, the Lord revealed himself as filled with goodness towards him —he promised to be with him, and to help him to speak.

By delivering his people out of mercy the Lord punished Pharaoh, and by this very act of such wonderful mercy to his people of Israel is shown sterner and sterner justice to Pharaoh. This justice appears in full force at the time of the Pasch when the destroying angel passed over, at the time of the passage over the Red Sea (Exod. 11. 4; 12. 29; 14. 15, etc.).

The wanderings of the people of Israel in the desert under God's guidance is marked by acts of mercy of the Lord, who watches over his people, but it is also marked by a series of punishments and acts of divine justice, calling Israel back to the right path, whenever the people murmured and wished to turn back (Exod. 15. 23). These wanderings under God's guidance make a wonderful spiritual journey, showing us how God, in his wisdom, in a marvellous way adjusts his mercies, his trials or his punishments. This is shown very clearly in the first stage, when they came to Mara. After three days in the desert without finding any wells, an oasis was reached, but its water was too bitter to drink. Here is the trial. The people murmured, and God, having compassion on them, by means of Moses changed the bitter water into sweet water, and he declared: "I am the Lord, and it is health I bring thee" (Exod. 15. 26). The Lord, however, made it plain that he would not show this mercy, unless the people did what was right in his eyes, and listened to his commandments and obeyed his laws.

This mercy was also shown when Moses was given the Ten Commandments on Mount Sinaï. It was an act of

mercy to wish to train the people of Israel once again, to
make them appreciate their religion, to teach them to
worship, but to train them by giving them the law was a
striking act of justice. All this Moses acknowledges in his
great canticle: "how perfect is all he [the Lord] does,
how right are all his dealings" (Deut. 32. 4). The purpose
of justice is to render to each man his due. Justice consid-
ers what is right. Moses adds: "God, faithful and unerr-
ing, God, holy and just" (Deut. 32. 4). But he is also
merciful, and so can declare:

> He sought them out in the wilderness, there in the fear-
> ful desert spaces, gave them the guidance, taught them the
> lessons they needed, guarded them as if they had been the
> apple of his eye. (So the eagle that would incite its young
> to venture in the air now hovers about them, now spreads
> its wings and takes them up to rest on its shoulders.) None
> but the Lord was their guide on that journey, there was no
> alien god to be found then in their company. And after-
> wards he settled them in a country of high hills, where
> they could eat the food their own lands yielded. (Deut. 32.
> 10–13.)

The prophets never cease to proclaim, to recall and to
sing of, the mercy and justice which characterize the
works of the Lord. I will quote only the more important
passages, which take us deeper into this mystery.

In her canticle of thanksgiving Anna acknowledges
that the Lord is a God of justice and mercy:

> The Lord is God all-knowing, and overrules the devices
> of men. See how he breaks the great warrior's bow, girds
> the feeble with strength; how the rich, for very need, must
> work as hirelings, while the hungry eat to their heart's con-
> tent! See how at last the barren womb bears many, and the
> fruitful mother is left to languish! Lord of death and life,
> he brings men to the grave and back from the grave; Lord
> of poverty and of wealth, he alone humbles, raising up the
> poor man out of the dust, the beggar from his dung-hill to
> sit among princes and reach the honours of a throne. [. . .]

The Lord will sit in judgement on the remotest people of earth. (1 Kings 2. 10.)

In Psalm 88 the glory and power of the Lord are praised and we are told "right and justice are the pillars of thy throne; mercy and faithfulness the heralds of thy country" (Ps. 88. 15).

In Psalms 9, 24 and 118 we find the theme developed at length:

But the Lord abides for ever on the throne of judgement he has prepared, still judging the world rightly, still awarding each people its due; the Lord is a stronghold to the oppressed, a stronghold in time of peril. Those who acknowledge thy name, Lord, can trust thee; never was man forsaken that had recourse to thee. [. . .] Have pity on me, Lord, look upon all that I suffer at my enemies' hands. [. . .] Now it will be seen how the Lord defends the right, how the wicked continue their own undoing. [. . .] He does not forget the helpless; their time will come; the patience of the afflicted will not go for nothing. [. . .] The destitute are cast on no care but thine; to thee only the orphan looks for redress. (Ps. 9. 8–11, 14, 17, 19, 35.)

How gracious is the Lord, how faithful, guiding our strayed feet back to the path! In his own laws he will train the humble, in his own paths the humble he will guide. [. . .] Kindly be thy judgement of my sin, for thy own honour's sake, my grievous sin. [. . .] Restless and forlorn I claim thy pity, to my sins be merciful. [. . .] Take my soul into thy keeping; come to my rescue, do not let me be disappointed of my trust in thee, uprightness and purity be my shield, as I wait, patiently, Lord, for thy help. (Ps. 24. 8–9, 11, 18, 20–21.)

So just, Lord, thou art, thy awards so truly given! [. . .] Stands thy faithfulness eternally, thy law for ever changeless. [. . .] Unblessed is my lot; look down and rescue me, that still am mindful of thy law. (Ps. 118. 137, 143, 153.

In Jeremias, Osee and Ezechiel the mercy of the Lord is shown with special tenderness. Speaking of Jacob, the Lord says:

Then I will heal that scar of thine, cure thee of thy wounds. [. . .] Nay, says the Lord, I mean to bring tent-dwelling Jacob home, have pity on those ruined wells, build the city anew on its height, set up the temple and its ordinances anew; here songs of praise shall echo once again, and cries of mirth. They shall increase, that hitherto had dwindled, be exalted, that once were brought low. [. . .] He who scattered Israel will gather Israel in, will guard it faithfully as a shepherd guards his flock. The Lord means to ransom Jacob, to grant deliverance from the tyrant's power. [. . .] I will turn all their sorrow into joy, comfort and cheer their sad hearts. (Jer. 30. 17; 30. 18–19; 31. 10–11.)

I will bring healing to their crushed spirits; in free mercy I will give them back my love; my vengeance has passed them by. I will be morning dew, to make Israel grow as the lilies grow, strike roots deep as the forest of Lebanon. These branches shall spread.

All at once my heart misgives me, and from its embers pity revives. And should I wreak my vengeance, of Ephraim take full toll? (Osee 14. 5–7; 11: 8–9.)

I mean to go on looking for this flock of mine, search it out for myself [. . .] so will I go looking for these sheep of mine, rescue them from all the nooks into which they have strayed when the dark mist fell upon them. [. . .] Yes, I will lead them out into fair pastures, the high mountains of Israel shall be their feeding-ground, the mountains of Israel, with soft grass for them to rest on, rich feed for them to graze. [. . .] The lost sheep I will find, the strayed sheep I will bring home again; bind up the broken limb, nourish the wasted form, keep the well-fed and the sturdy free from harm; they shall have a true shepherd at last. (Ezech. 34. 11–16.)

Isaias announces the glorious future of Israel:

The Lord our judge, the Lord our lawgiver, the Lord our king, will himself be our deliverance . . . then, thou wilt have the spoil of many forays to divide, even lame folk shall carry plunder away. No more shall they cry out on their helpless plight, these, thy fellow citizens; none dwells there now but is assoiled of his guilt. [. . .] It is I, still it is I, that will bring thee consolation. (Isaias 33. 22–4; 51. 12.)

The sacrifice of the cross is supremely a work of the "uprightness" of the Father, and a work of his mercy; the two are intimately connected. The sacrifice of the cross is the supreme work of justice. The justice of God is never so pure, so strict, so exact, as on the cross. When it is applied to the sinner, he is incapable of enduring the strict justice of God, for he is incapable of making amends for the offence against God and his love which is a consequence of the sin he has freely committed, in his pride and disobedience.

The justice of God could be applied perfectly to Christ, the Man-God, infinitely pure, but out of mercy taking upon himself all the sins of the world. In strict justice Jesus can make amends for all the offences of mankind, because he is the Incarnate Word, and therefore God. All the deaths Jesus suffered during the agony, on the cross, in the burial, he endured heroically, with an extraordinary intensity and awareness; all these deaths were punishment due to the sins of men, which he was willing to bear as if they were his own punishment, as if he, the just one, really deserved them. He bore them in order to satisfy God's justice, in order to pay the terrible debt of sinful humanity, of the woman who was unfaithful and an adulteress, to use the symbolism of Scripture. By his willingness to satisfy every demand of justice in full, Jesus crucified shows us the greatness and gravity of God's justice, which is in no way arbitrary, but is the wisdom of God. By this means Jesus makes us understand more clearly the enormity of the sin which opposes and despises this justice. Jesus loves justice, and the Father's law. By being crucified he became its defender. Not a jot of the law must be lost, for it is written on stone by the finger of God. The Pharisees are false defenders of the law and of God's justice, for they defend it in its literal meaning, its material application, without concerning themselves with

the spirit that gives it life, or with the intentions of those
who obey it. To them the essential thing is that the law
should be applied, and that no external reproach should
be possible. They make out of it a kind of artistic standard
for their lives. Jesus respects the law and defends it, by
living according to its spirit, by making his intention con-
form to that of the lawgiver. Hence he truly fulfils it in
his sacrifice on the Cross.

For in this the purpose of the law was realized in a
higher way: the people of Israel by means of Jesus crucified worshipped God in a supreme fashion; all the commandments are supremely carried out in Jesus crucified.
Hence the law is fulfilled through the crucifixion, and has
no further reason to exist.[3]

The resurrection of Christ's body, which had been
hidden in the sepulchre, is the supreme work of justice of
the great Judge, giving to every man his due. To Christ
crucified, to the Lamb who was slain, is due the glorification of the resurrection; to Christ crucified, who had experienced poverty and humiliation to the full, is due in
virtue of divine justice the wonderful and everlasting exaltation on the night of the Pasch. To the wounded, humiliated heart of Christ crucified is due that immense exaltation and glorification. The risen heart of the Lamb
is the source of all the light of the heavenly Jerusalem.

This supreme work of the Father's "uprightness" allows
us to reflect on this "uprightness" of God. God is just, and
is justice. By saying this we express an attribute of God,
one of the qualities of his will and of his being. We imply
indeed that God gives to each one his due, while understanding that God owes nothing to any creature, but in
creating them gives them all that their being requires, that
they may share as perfectly as possible in his goodness.

[3] What is true of the cross remains true of all the other activities
of Christ from the time of his conception.

To be just is, for God, to bring about that order which wisdom has willed in all things, an order expressed and proclaimed by the law. The justice of the Father is manifested on the cross, just because Christ made amends for sins, re-established the order upset by disobedience, just because Christ fulfilled the law by his obedience.

Again, justice is shown in the resurrection because it carries out what is due to Christ crucified. The sacrifice of the cross is the supreme work of God's mercy, of a mercy which is exercised in a sweet and gracious manner. God wishes to save mankind, to forgive their sins by means of one among themselves, of him who is "King" of mankind, and who, being both God and man, can make amends for all his brethren, as the Lord wished to save his people by means of Moses and Aaron.

Further, he wishes to unite in the closest way the friends of Christ to the mystery of his redemption. Jesus does not live the mystery of his agony, his crucifixion and his burial by himself alone, but he does so in union with his Mother, with John, and the holy women, indeed with all his disciples, and all those who are willing, freely and lovingly, to be his disciples. This, too, is an act of mercy and overflowing love. For, from the standpoint of justice, the sacrifice of Christ is fully and perfectly sufficient. It is perfect, and effects perfect redemption. Mary was asked to become associated in it not in order to complete Christ's work of reparation and satisfaction, as though something was lacking in him, but in order to carry out his overflowing mercy. To allow Mary to cooperate in her Son's work and to live by its means is to allow her to share a new relationship and more perfect friendship with him. Perfect friendship requires this friendly cooperation, since friends are associated together by doing the same work.

Then, the sacrifice of the cross is the supreme work of God's mercy just because this sacrifice, while a work of filial worship, is also a means to free men from sin, the merciful gift of Christ to his brethren, to those whom he has come to redeem. The mystery of the Eucharist expresses and fulfils this gift in the truest and most effective way. Christ wishes to give himself to us under the form of bread and wine, as our food and drink. The Eucharist continues for us the cross. The merciful gift of Christ, giving himself to his members, is also the gift which the Father makes to us of his beloved Son. The Father makes this gift to those who have refused to obey him, who have offended him, and crucified his Son, who have revolted against his law and his will. He is not contented with forgiving their sins, but wishes to make use of these pardoned sins in order to give them more love, to communicate to them in full the divine life. The liturgy does not hesitate to sing "happy fault, which has given us such a saviour." That is how the mercy of Christ, the Good Shepherd of his sheep, and especially of the lost sheep, reveals to us the mercy of God, the Father of all mercy, himself, above all, the Good Shepherd. The parable of the prodigal son shows us the mercy of the Father, receiving back the prodigal, forgiving him, embracing him, clothing him with the marriage garment, killing the fatted calf (Luke 15. 11–32). That is how the Father receives his prodigals, his younger sons, on the cross. Sinners are clothed anew through the royal blood of Christ, are fed with his body and his heart; were it possible the good angels—the elder sons—who are always in the Father's house, would be jealous.

By the sacrifice of the cross we can, then, contemplate the mystery of God's fatherly mercy, unveiling God's over-flowing goodness and love. To say that a person is merciful is not only to say that he is good, but that he is good in such a way as to comfort the misery of those around him; it is to express a full, perfect, overflowing goodness. Mercy can only be used to describe one who is high in the order of goodness. Hence mercy is only true perfectly of God, for God is highest in the order of goodness, supreme and infinite in goodness.

By declaring that God is merciful I bear witness that God's goodness is such that he can give help in every misery. He is ever able to get rid of the cause of all troubles, sin. Not only is God capable, by his goodness, of getting rid of all troubles, but he will get rid of them, when he wills it. On the cross God forgave all the sins of mankind. God is not only merciful, but he is Mercy, and Forgiveness, as he is Love, that is, he is the source of all mercy and forgiveness, and all mercy and forgiveness come from him. Therefore the mystery of Christ crucified and the mystery of the Eucharist are the direct results, the masterpieces of this fatherly mercy.

Reconciliation in God of mercy and justice

It is primarily in the mystery of Christ crucified that harmony is perfectly established between God's mercy and justice. In the Old Testament for the most part we find both works of justice and works of mercy. This is particularly clear in the story of Moses: on the one hand the Lord wishes to free his people and save them, and, on the other hand, the Lord punishes Pharaoh, exercising justice towards him. On the cross the justice of God is shown in full vigour upon Christ suffering and crucified, and at the same time the fullness of mercy is also shown to Christ. Hence the psalm tells us: "See where mercy and faithfulness meet in one; how justice and peace are united in one embrace! Faithfulness grows up out of the earth, and from heaven, redress looks down" (Ps. 84. 11–12).

Justice, however strict, is wrapped up in mercy; it is wholly dependent on mercy, which comes first. Christ, out of mercy, is willing to be the Lamb of God, clothed with all the consequences of our sins. Justice is wholly directed towards mercy, mercy coming as the final end. Everything is accomplished in mercy. We may say that justice, even in its strict sense, is at the service of mercy. allowing it to be what it is, and to flourish in a marvellous degree. If Christ had not satisfied for the sins of men, the mercy of the Father could not have been exercised towards him so abundantly. He would not be our Saviour; he would not have given himself up in this way for each of us.

This connection between justice and mercy, manifested so plainly on the cross, perhaps makes us understand better how the wisdom of God's government is shown in regard to Christ and his mystical body. God's wisdom is a wisdom of love and mercy, making use of justice and the law in order to become pure and complete.

Thus we can contemplate the mystery of God's wisdom, mercy and justice. In God these qualities are not indeed distinct in the way they are in man, when they balance one another. In God they are identical with his being: God *is* wisdom, justice and mercy. Hence each of these qualities only exist in God in a perfect way, without, however, limiting one another. God is not sheer justice, "justice in itself," but he is justice, mercy and wisdom.

While, as regards the works of God, we can speak of a reconciliation in God's acts between mercy and justice, in God himself there is not merely harmony between them, but formal identity. Justice as applied to the being of God, which is God, far from involving any contradiction to his mercy, is formally identified with his mercy. In this lies the mystery of the perfection of God's being, containing in a higher way all the perfections which apply to the creature, not in the sense of a sum of these perfections, or of a whole of which they are parts, but as possessing them in a higher unity, in absolute simplicity. The perfection of God's being is such that in God justice and mercy are identified.

Thus it is not surprising that all the works of God are justice and mercy, that all his works reflect his justice and mercy. Some reflect one more clearly, others reflect the other more clearly.

For this reason some of the works of God are called works of justice, others works of mercy, but all reflect him who is justice and mercy in wisdom.

THE SACRIFICE OF THE CROSS: THE REVELATION OF THE FATHER'S OMNIPOTENCE, AND OF HIS PRESENCE IN ALL THAT EXISTS

Now, it belongs to God on high, almighty and truly God, to be everywhere, to watch over all and know all. He is not contained in any place, for then the place which contained him would be greater than that which was contained. God is not contained, but he is the place containing everything (Theophilus of Antioch, *ad Autolycum*, 2, 3).

God, one, uncreated, eternal, invisible, impassible, incomprehensible, unlimited, understood by spirit and reason alone, clothed in light, beauty, spirit, of unspeakable power, through whom all has come to have being (Athenagoras, *Apology*, 10, 1).

The act of worship puts man in the presence of his Creator, whose first quality is omnipotence. To create, in the strict sense, requires infinite power, at least if the act of creation consists in giving being without any pre-existing reality, that is from nothing. To create is to give reality to a being, starting from nothing.

Every action presupposes a certain active power in him who exercises this action. The quality proper to this action manifests the quality proper to the power which it demands. Now the quality proper to this primary act, on which all others depend, is unique. This action is an action which has no need of support, of matter, in order to exist, but which communicates being to its proper effect. This act of creation, therefore, presupposes a unique power, a power wholly active. The omnipotence of God expresses such power, entirely unlimited, since its purpose is, directly, being. It affects, it can affect, all that exists, all that can exist. Hence the quality proper to the Creator is to be one who acts upon being, who is almighty.

It is thus that God presents himself to Abraham: "I am El Shaddaï, God Almighty; live as in my sight, and be perfect." [4]

The name, El Shaddaï, seems to be the most primitive name given to God.[5] This seems to confirm the traditional meaning of "God almighty."

The first and fundamental revelation made to us in Scripture about God's mystery is concerned with his creative activity. He is God, Creator of heaven and earth.[6] We are shown the splendour of his work, how great and harmonious it is, in order that we may be able to know from this the power and greatness of him who made it. To man, created in his image and likeness, God has given power to rule over the fishes and birds. By this power he is like the Creator; by worship, the offering of first-fruits, of the fruits of the earth and of his flocks, two kinds of fruitfulness, man acknowledges that

[4] Gen. 17. 1. The text "I am El Shaddaï" is rendered by the Vulgate, *Ego Deus omnipotens*. Some scholars at the present day think that the translation of El Shaddaï by "God almighty" is inaccurate; probably it means: the God of the mountains: cf. Gen. 28. 3; 35. 1; 43. 14; 48. 3; Num. 24. 4.

[5] Exod. 6. 2: God said to Moses: "I am the same Lord who revealed myself to Abraham, Isaac and Jacob; but although I revealed myself as El Shaddaï, my name Adonai I did not make known to them"

[6] Gen. 1. 1: "God, at the beginning of time, created heaven and earth." Heaven and earth are God's works, they come from him, God is before them.

he is wholly dependent on the Creator, that his work can do nothing at all except through the help of God's omnipotence. It is entirely to be expected that the sacrifice of worship, that first and fundamental act of religious life for man, should be concerned with what is fundamental and first in the revelation of God's mystery: his omnipotence as Creator.

Each of the great sacrifices, described in the Old Testament and mentioned here, reveals directly to us an aspect of the mystery of God's omnipotence. The sacrifice of Abel reveals to us above all the power of him who is the source of all fruitfulness, lord of life and death. The sacrifice of Noah shows us the omnipotence of him who, master of the human race and its destiny, master of the world, can, when he wishes, make use of the elements in the universe. The sacrifice of Abraham reveals to us the omnipotence of him who is greater than his gifts, however wonderful they may be, of him who is dependent on none of these gifts: he can, if he chooses and judges it right, demand that they be offered up. The sacrifice of the Pasch reveals to us the omnipotence of him who in some sense is able to create afresh the people of Israel, to give them their freedom and their true calling, in spite of the power of Pharaoh—in comparison with the omnipotence of God the power of Pharaoh is nothing. The sacrifice of Elias manifests clearly the omnipotence of the true God, omnipotence put at the service of prayer and worship, and vouches for its power. It is an omnipotence of fire, of love; that is, an omnipotence which listens to the prayer of those who call upon it, and grants their request. The sacrifice of the seven brothers and of their mother manifests the omnipotence of him who is able to give back life, to raise the dead.

While all true sacrifice makes man nothing in the presence of the mystery of his Creator's omnipotence and, while this making him nothing can give him an intimate realization of God's omnipotence, the praises, the canticles we find in Scripture declare God's omnipotence and, further, give us striking accounts of this mystery.

Some passages, therefore, may be quoted here. In the Canticle of Moses after the departure from Egypt the omnipotence of the Lord is acknowledged and praised:

> That power could hurl Pharao's chariots, Pharao's army, into the sea; drowned in the Red Sea, the flower of all his chivalry; the depths closed over them, and they sank to the bottom like a stone. How magnificent, Lord, is the strength of thy right hand; that right hand which has shattered the enemy! Against such majesty rose they but to fall; the hot breath of thy anger burnt them up like stubble. The waters were piled high through the blast of thy fury; the waves were still, at the sea's heart the depths congealed. [. . .] [The boldest plans of the enemy were nothing before the power of the Lord.] A breath from thee, and the sea closed over them; they sank in the raging waters like lead. What power is there, Lord, that can match thee? Who, as thou art, is august in holiness, who so worthy of fear and of praise, who so wonderful in his doings? Thou hadst but to stretch out thy hand, and the earth swallowed them up. [. . .] Still as a stone, under the threat of thy powerful arm, they must watch thy people go by. (Exod. 15. 4–8, 10–12, 16.)

As fire is the symbol of love and anger, so the arm of the Lord, or his hand, symbolizes his power (Exod. 32. 11: Moses, addressing the Lord, asks him to remember his people, whom "thou didst rescue from Egypt so imperiously, with so strong a hand").

In the Canticle of Moses just before his death the Lord's power does not cease to be declared, as, too, in that first Magnificat, the canticle of Anna. The power of the Lord is praised in the psalms and prophets. This absolute omnipotence, which nothing can resist, which can give life and can give death, is always considered as belonging to the true God, to the Lord, alone. Idols, false gods, have no power.

It is mine to kill and to quicken, mine to smite and to heal; from my power there is no deliverance [Deut. 32. 39]. Lord of death and life, he brings men to the grave and back from the grave [1 Kings 2. 6]. The Lord will strike terror into his adversaries; hark, how his thunders roll above them in heaven [1 Kings 3. 10]. The Lord is my rock-fastness, my bulwark, my rescuer. It is my God that brings me aid, and gives me confidence; he is my shield, my weapon of deliverance, my protector, my stronghold; he it is that preserves me and frees me from wrong. Praised be the Lord! When I invoke him I am secure from my enemies. [. . . The wrath of the Lord shakes the foundations of the world:]

He bade heaven stoop, and came down to earth, with mist at his feet; he came, mounted on the cherubim, borne up on the wings of the wind, shrouded in a pall of darkness, wringing out the rainstorm from the clouds of heaven; burning coals were kindled by the lightning that went before him; the Lord, sending his thunder from heaven, the Most High, letting his voice be heard. How they scattered when he rained down his arrows on them, fled in confusion before his lightning! The secret springs of ocean came to light, the very foundations of the world were laid bare, when the Lord threatened them, blew upon them with the breath of his anger. (2 Kings 22. 2–4, 10–16.)

And are not those heavens, Lord, witnesses of thy wonderful power [. . .] Lord God of hosts, who can compare with thee; in this power, Lord, that is thine, in the faithfulness that everywhere attends thee? It is thou that dost curb this pride of the sea, and calm the tumult of its waves; wounded lies Rahab at thy feet, by the strong arm that has routed thy enemies. [Ps. 88. 6, 9–11; *Rahab* is the name of a mythical monster personifying the sea. Cf. Job 7. 12. It also signified Egypt.] And wilt thou bring man to dust again, that thou sayest, Return, children of Adam, to what you were? . . . Swiftly thou bearest our lives away, as a waking dream, or the green grass that blooms fresh with the morning; night finds it faded and dead. Still thy anger takes toll of us, thy displeasure denies us rest, so jealous thy scrutiny of our wrong-doing, so clear our hidden sins shew in the light of thy presence [Ps. 89. 3, 5–8]. The Lord reigns as King, robed in majesty; royalty the Lord has for robe and girdle. He it was that founded the solid earth, to abide immovable. Firm stood thy throne ere ever the world began; from all eternity, thou art [Ps. 92. 1–2].

There lies the vast ocean, stretching wide on every hand; this, too, is peopled with living things past number, great creatures and small; the ships pass them on their course. Leviathan himself is among them; him, too, thou hast created to roam there at his pleasure. And all look to thee to send them their food at the appointed time; it is through thy gift they find it, thy hand opens, and all are filled with content. But see, thou hidest thy face, and they are dismayed; thou takest their life from them, and they breathe no more, go back to the dust they came from. Then thou sendest forth thy spirit, and there is fresh creation; thou dost repeople the face of the earth. (Ps. 103. 25–30.)

Recount we now what things the Lord has made; his visible creation be our theme; nothing he has fashioned but hangs on his word. (Ecclus. 42. 15.)

If the great deeds of God in the past enable us to contemplate his power, the future, which must come, enables us to do so still better. The prophets, who announce the coming of the Lord, praise the splendour of his majesty. The omnipotence of the Lord will then appear with a splendour hitherto unknown. Then we shall understand that he alone is worthy to be exalted above all (Isaias 2, 6–22). But before this coming the terrible wrath of the Lord will be shown. These occasions, in their own way, show his power by revealing his supreme authority. All authority requires a certain power, and supreme authority requires absolute power.[7]

"Look, you, the Lord means to make earth a void, a wilderness; twist it out of shape, and scatter its inhabitants far and wide" (Isaias 24. 1). "The flood-gates of heaven will be opened, and the foundations of the earth rock;

[7] It would be interesting to analyse the different occasions of the wrath of the Lord recorded by Scripture. These occasions reveal different aspects of the authority of God, who has been offended by the sins of men. They give us a better understanding of certain aspects of God's omnipotence.

earth must be rent and riven, earth torn and tattered, earth must quiver and quake; earth rolling and reeling like a drunkard, earth tottering like some frail shelter that is gone in a night, bowed down by the weight of its own guilt, till it falls, never to rise again" (Isaias 24. 18–20).

The sacrifice of Christ and his resurrection reveal to us in a fresh way, and yet in continuation of the Old Testament revelation, the mystery of God's omnipotence. As a sacrifice of love, containing in a higher way the perfections of all the sacrifices of the Old Testament, the sacrifice of the cross shows us, as they do, every aspect of the mystery of God's omnipotence. Through his act of worship Jesus acknowledges that everything that exists comes from God and depends on him, that nothing can occur without his almighty will. Jesus entirely surrenders his human will to the will of the Father. He offers to the Father his own human will in order to glorify that of the Father.

By his complete surrender of his own will Jesus pays homage to the supreme majesty of the Father. Control of his human nature, of the image of God, is allowed to give way before that of God, of God's omnipotence. Thus he declares the supreme rights of his God over himself, over the whole human race, over the whole universe, which he rules. Through him the whole human race, the whole universe honours, in its head, the almighty majesty of God. We see, then, how the greatness of the sacrifice manifests, beyond any other, the omnipotence of God. The greater the value of the victim offered to God the more the rights of God and his omnipotence are glorified by the offering. The Lamb of God, offered up at the agony and on the cross, possesses supreme and incomparable value; he is the true Isaac, the well-beloved son, not only of the patriarch Abraham, but of the whole human race, the true Isaac of mankind. He is that supreme one, who is offered on the mountain to make us under-

stand the absolute claim of God's will, the omnipotence
of his will, which has right of life and death. This Son of
the promise given to Mary and to men is taken back by
the Father when he wills. Men would have liked to make
a human use of the divine gift of the Son, to enhance their
own temporal glory. The Father takes him back to make
us understand the divine way in which we should use his
gift of Love, to make us understand the omnipotence of
his love, which is accountable to no one, but which remains faithful amid the infidelities of men.

The Father takes back him whom men have rejected,
in order to give him in a still more wonderful way. His
omnipotence is truly an omnipotence of love, unwearying,
unchangeable and faithful.

When Pilate at the Pretorium, astonished by the silence of Jesus, asked him: "Dost thou not know that I
have power to crucify thee, and power to release thee?"
Jesus replied: "Thou wouldst not have any power over
me at all, if it had not been given thee from above" (John
19. 10–11). And he died, expressing his absolute trust in
the loving omnipotence of the Father: "Father, into thy
hands I commend my spirit" (Luke 23. 46).

His worship, being a filial worship of love, reveals to
us in a fresh way the omnipotence of the Father's love;
indeed, it is always the same mystery of the Creator's
omnipotence which is declared and manifested, as certain
outward facts make clear: "Then was darkness over all
the earth until the ninth hour" (Luke 23. 44).

"All at once the veil of the temple was torn this way
and that from the top to the bottom, and the earth shook,
and the rocks parted asunder, and the graves were opened"
(Matt. 27. 51–2).

This sacrifice bears witness, as did that of Elias on
Mount Carmel, that the Lord is the only true God, and
that he who had just committed his soul into the hands of

the Father was the holy one of God, his messenger, whom men have not received. The centurion gave glory to God: "This was indeed a just man. And the whole multitude of those who stood there watching it, when they saw the issue, went home beating their breasts" (Luke 23. 47–8).

Above all, however, in this sacrifice it is the power of the Father's love which is manifested; it is God's fatherly omnipotence, the omnipotence of his loving heart, which is revealed. Thus a much more inward and profound aspect of the mystery of God's omnipotence is reached, and communicated to us. In order to get a clear grasp of these two aspects of the mystery we should have to compare the theophanies of the Old Testament, and that of the nativity. In the Old Testament the theophanies were usually accompanied by plain, visible, manifestations, witnessing to the omnipotence of the Creator-God. We have only to think of the great theophany of Mount Sinaï. It is truly the omnipotence of the Creator, the majesty of the Lord, King of the universe, which is manifested.

In the New Testament God at first comes to dwell among us without any external manifestation. Only the *fiat* of Mary, who lives unknown, is demanded. The virgin motherhood of Mary, miraculous indeed, but concealed by the presence of Joseph, is the means, employed by God's wisdom, for his new presence among men. God comes to dwell among us, to share our home, taking possession of our earth in the most delicate, yet effective way; he springs indeed from Mary and, through her, from the human race. Yet all remains hidden, veiled, silent. . . . No one but Mary can know of it. It is not a passing theophany, but a dwelling among us which is secret, intimate, and complete, a taking possession for ever of human nature by God himself. Human nature is assumed by God, and becomes his secret, hidden, temple, *in sinu Mariae*.

At the nativity God is seen with the characteristics of a young child, looking at his mother who loves him. The almighty hand of God, his arm, is seen in and through the delicate hand of a small child, the weak arm of a child.

This wonderful theophany, more extraordinary than that of Mount Sinaï, takes place in the silence of the night, in a poor stable, a shelter for cattle, in solitude. The omnipotence of God, the Creator, is veiled under the appearance of a little child, in order to show only the most intimate love. Nothing more is seen, it is wholly for the sake of love, hiding under a child's feeble ways in order to let love have full scope. The singing of the angels, the star of the Magi, the miraculous birth of Jesus, tell us that the omnipotence of God is at work, that it is present and is active, but that it acts in the shadow of love, fulfilling the demands of silence, of intimacy, of friendship.

It is not surprising that on the cross we find this same law of God's government: love does all, omnipotence is present, it acts in a divine way to allow love to take all. Here, again, the mystery of the Eucharist helps us to understand the cross. In this mystery the omnipotence of the Creator is present and active; it performs the amazing miracle of transubstantiation (the substance of the bread is changed into the substance of Christ's body), but it is all for the sake of the gift of love, allowing love to be given us as bread, the nourishment which we use the most. On the cross omnipotence is at work to allow the Lamb to be a victim of love to the fullest extent, to allow the heart of Jesus to be the final victim. It is indeed the revelation of the loving omnipotence of the Father, King over hearts, King over the secrets of hearts, which is manifested to us. The majesty of God is not only that of the Creator, but above all it is the majesty of the Father, of him who is love, it is the majesty and triumph of love. The authority and omnipotence of God are not only those of the Creator, but they are above all those of the Father, of him who is love. It is the authority and omnipotence of love. Hence this majesty, this authority, this omnipotence, cannot be further manifested by outward, extraordinary signs, but they can only be manifested simply and intimately, and amid poverty.

In the mystery of the resurrection these two aspects of the mystery of God's omnipotence, which complete one another—the omnipotence of the Creator and that of the Father—are both found to be present. The resurrection is the work of a creative omnipotence, which creates everything anew, and it is also the work of an omnipotence of love; all is created anew, to glorify and manifest love. The glorified body of the risen Jesus is the living monstrance of his love for the Father and for us. His body is the splendour of the Son's love for the Father and for us. It is a new creation through love, a direct source of love, filled with the light of love. The omnipotence of the Father is at work there; it is his masterpiece of beauty and of love.

Thus we can understand better how omnipotence and love are but one in God. Omnipotence and love are identical. Nevertheless, when we say that God is almighty, we express a different meaning from what we express by saying that God is love. To declare that God is almighty is to assert that he depends on no one, and that everything depends on him, that he can accomplish what he wills in his wisdom. For this reason Scripture tells us that to God all things are possible. God can always do what he wills, for this is always in accordance with his wisdom. Hence, his absolute power, which belongs to the first cause, expresses, above all, the sovereign power to rule: everything depends ultimately on him, and he can depend on no one, for he is first.

The almighty power, which characterizes the first cause, lets us grasp the absolute autonomy of God. Yet we must never separate in God the omnipotence which characterizes the first cause and the omnipotence of love. For in God his love is his being, and his being is his love. The sovereign rule of God is a sovereign rule of one who is love. God is almighty love, as he is almighty being. In every creature there is a real distinction between power and love, though in the ordinary course there is no opposition between these two qualities, but a due order. Power is directed towards love, and presupposes it. It is, as it were, wrapped in love. Sin at first introduces a certain opposition between these qualities, between the order of the affective and that of the efficient, and inverts the order willed by God. The sinner puts love at the service of the efficient. Then man is no longer the image of God, but the image of Lucifer, who loves no longer, but seeks to "do," who now lives only in the desire to bring about a new world. He believes he is the prince of this world.

We might suppose that, on account of the sovereign majesty of his omnipotence, God is far from creatures, far from the heart and understanding of man. It is true that certain statements in Scripture might make us think that God, at certain moments, is far from his creatures, while at other moments he is near them.

Solomon, after building the temple to be the house of God, asked the question: "Folly it were to think that God has a dwelling-place on earth. If the very heavens, and the heavens that are above the heavens, cannot contain thee, what welcome can it offer thee, this house, which I have built? Yet, O Lord my God, do not let this prayer go all unheeded, that sues for thy favour; listen to the cry of entreaty thy servant makes before thee this day!" (3 Kings 8. 27–8).

In the psalms we often find an appeal, expressing the fear that God is far away, hidden from him who invokes him:

"O Lord, hear my prayer, and let my cry come unto thee. Do not turn thy face away from me, but lend me thy ear in time of affliction; give me swift audience whenever I call upon thee" (Ps. 101. 2–3). "Lord, why dost thou stand far off? In days of affliction, why dost thou make no sign?" (Ps. 9. 22). "Lord, must I still go all unremembered, must thy look still be turned away from me?" (Ps. 12. 2). "My God, my God, why hast thou forsaken me?" (Ps. 21. 1).

This fear, which man experiences, seems to be justified by the very words of God. After Adam's sin the Lord sought him in the garden. Adam hid himself, and God called to him: "Where art thou?" as though God did not know where he was; on account of his omnipotent majesty it sometimes appears that God is remote from man.

Nevertheless, if we consider the mystery of his majesty and omnipotence, that of God as Creator as well as that of God the Father, we can easily understand that, through his almighty power, God can be present in a unique and intimate way to all that can exist, and that he is in fact present to all that exists. The mystery of worship makes us live in his presence. Scripture reveals to us this presence of God in all his works in a clear and often striking way. Some specially significant passages may be quoted here.

God appeared to Jacob in a dream, and told him: "I myself will watch over thee wherever thou goest, and bring thee back to this land again; before I have done with thee, all my promises to thee shall be fulfilled." Jacob, waking up, cried out: "Why, this is the Lord's dwelling-place, and I slept here unaware of it" (Gen. 28. 15–16).

God appeared to Moses, as having taken possession of the place, when he appeared, and this ground was "holy" (Exod. 3. 5). God said he had seen the misery of the people of Israel, that he would be with Moses in the mission he entrusted to him. He gave him a sign that Moses might know of his presence.

Mount Sinaï, also, seemed a place where God dwelt: "Moses went up to meet God, and the voice of God came to him from the mountain" (Exod. 19. 3). "It was on the very top of Mount Sinaï that the Lord had come down, and now he called Moses up to the summit" (Exod. 19. 20).

The Lord told Moses to build him a sanctuary, that he might dwell among his people: "I mean them to build me a sanctuary, so that I can dwell among them" (Exod. 25. 8). This sanctuary was to possess an ark, in which Moses should place the written law. The Lord said: "Thence will I issue my commands; from that throne of mercy, between the two cherubs that stand over the ark and its records, my voice shall come to thee, whenever I send word through thee to the sons of Israel" (Exod. 25. 22). We can understand the words of the psalmist: "Who is it, Lord, that will make his home in thy tabernacle, rest on the mountain where thy sanctuary is?" (Ps. 14. 1).

When Israel was settled in the promised land, Solomon changed the sanctuary of the Lord into the temple, that it might be his house, his holy dwelling-place: "It is true, then, the house I have built is to be thy dwelling, thy throne for ever immovable" (3 Kings 8. 13).

Solomon, while asking the Lord in his prayer to fulfil his promise, and dwell in the temple built for the glory of his name, acknowledged that the heavens could not contain God. The psalm of David, praising the bounty of the Creator, is plain: "O Lord, our Master, how the majesty of thy name fills all the earth! Thy greatness is high above heaven itself. Thou hast made the lips of children, of infants at the breast, vocal with praise" (Ps. 8. 2–3).

The Lord answered the prayer of Solomon: "This temple thou hast built I myself have hallowed, to be the everlasting shrine of my name; never a day but my eyes shall be watching, my heart attentive here. . . . But if you and your children are content to turn your backs on me, following me no more, neglecting the commands and observances I have enjoined on you . . . this temple I have hallowed as the shrine of my name, shall be thrust away out of my sight. Israel shall become a proverb and a byword among all the nations" (3 Kings 9. 3, 6–7).

The fact that the temple was the principal liturgical sanctuary where God dwelt did not prevent God from continuing to appear to whom he willed, and where he willed. This is plain in the lives of the prophets, and an example is God's meeting with Elias. Elias fled in fear to the desert to save his life, and then he begged the Lord to come and take him. The Lord commanded him to go to Mount Horeb:

> Then word came to him to go out and stand there in the Lord's presence; the Lord God himself would pass by. A wind there was, rude and boisterous, that shook the mountains and broke the rocks in pieces before the Lord, but the Lord was not in the wind. And after the wind, an earthquake, but the Lord was not in the earthquake. And after the earthquake a fire, but the Lord was not in the fire. And after the fire, the whisper of a gentle breeze. Elias, when he heard it, wrapped his face in his mantle, and went out to stand at the cave door. Then a voice came to him. (3 Kings 19. 11–13.)

Though the Lord seemed to go and dwell in certain places, one after the other, without however being limited by these places, though these places were at first natural "high places" and later built by the people of God, yet, in the psalms, God himself is regarded as a place of refuge for the poor and the wretched; he is a strong place for those who fight.

The true sanctuary of the Lord is the Lord himself, who is above all we can conceive. The heaven of heavens is the true holy of holies. There are many passages in the psalms which express this clearly:

The Lord, who looks down from his sanctuary on high, viewing earth from heaven, who has listened to the groans of the prisoners, delivered a race that was doomed to die. [100. 20–1.] It was thou, Lord, that didst lay the foundations of earth when time began, it was thy hand that built the heavens. They will perish, but thou wilt remain; they will all be like a cloak that grows threadbare and thou wilt lay them aside like a garment, and exchange them for new; thou art unchanging, thy years can never fail. [101. 26–8.] The Lord is sovereign King of all the nations. Who is like the Lord our God, so high above us, that stoops to regard both heaven and earth [112. 4–6].

Yet, we must not suppose that God is far away, because he stoops to regard heaven and earth, and is above the heavens. God sees all, hears all, and lives in close contact with all that exists.

Is he deaf, the God who implanted hearing in us; is he blind, the God who gave us eyes to see? [93. 9.] The Lord looks into men's hearts, and finds there illusion. [93. 11.] Lord, I lie open to thy scrutiny; thou knowest when I sit down and when I rise up again, canst read my thoughts from far away. Walk I or sleep I, thou canst tell; no movement of mine but thou art watching it. Before ever the words are framed on my lips, all my thought is known to thee; rearguard and vanguard, thou dost compass me about, thy hand still laid upon me. [138. 1–5.] Where can I go, then, to take refuge from thy spirit, to hide from thy view? If I should climb up to heaven, thou art there; if I sink down to the world beneath, thou art present still. If I could wing my way eastwards, or find a dwelling beyond the western sea, still would I find thee beckoning to me, thy right hand upholding me. Or perhaps I would think to bury myself in darkness; night should surround me, friendlier than day; but no, darkness is no hiding-place from thee, with thee the night shines clear as day itself; light and dark are one. [138. 7–12.] Of my soul thou hast full knowledge, and this mortal frame had no mysteries for thee, who didst contrive it in secret, devise its pattern, there in the dark recesses of the earth. All my acts thy eyes have seen, all are set down already in thy record; my days were numbered before ever they came to be. [138. 15–16.]

This almighty knowledge of the Lord, this effective presence, unlimited, asserted so magnificently in the psalms of David, is asserted afresh by the prophets Jeremias (17. 9–10), Isaias (41. 10–31; 49. 16–26; 30. 1–3), Amos (9. 1–6), as well as in the book of Job (12–14), and the book of Wisdom (10 et seq.).

I need only quote the following passages from Isaias and Jeremias:

And now, here is a mesage from the Lord to Jacob, his creature, to the Israel he fashioned: Do not be afraid, I have bought thee for myself, and given thee the name thou bearest; thou belongest to me. Pass through water, and I will be with thee, so that the flood shall not drown thee; walk amid the flames, and thou shalt not be burnt, the fire shall have no power to catch thee. I am the Lord thy God, the Holy One of Israel, thy deliverer (Isaias 43. 1–3).

God am I, the Lord says, only when I stand near, and not when I am far away? Where, he would know, will you hide so close that he is not watching you, he, the Lord, that fills heaven and earth? (Jer. 23. 23–4).

With the mystery of the Incarnate Word the mystery of the presence of God in a place, in a sanctuary, in the temple, reached its final conclusion in a wonderful way. This new sanctuary was indeed Mary, in whom the mystery of the Incarnate Word was effected, this new presence of God among men, a presence at first hidden within Mary, the presence of the child to his mother. It was a visible presence of God as a child at the nativity, in poverty, mankind refusing to receive him—Mary, Joseph and the shepherds alone living in this wonderful presence.

God was then present to mankind as a child is present to its mother, as a child gives itself to its mother, to reveal to us how he is present to men, how he wishes to be Emmanuel, "God with us" (Matt. 1. 23). The whole hidden life of Jesus is a life of presence to Mary and Joseph, presence of God in the simplicity of daily family life.

The active presence of Christ in his apostolic life, to his disciples, by means of his miracles, preaching and teaching, is, again, a sign of the presence of the Father, who draws men, enlightens their minds and hearts, in order to bring them to the Father's house (cf. Luke 9. 28–36; Mark 9. 2–8; Matt. 17. 1–8: We should understand the mystery of the Transfiguration in the apostolic life of Christ as a mystery of presence).

Clearly, however, it is especially in the mystery of the crucifixion and of the resurrection that Christ reveals to us the mystery of the lasting, efficacious and loving presence of the Father to each of us and to the whole world. On the cross and in the resurrection he is indeed the sacrament of the Father's presence, as the mystery of the Eucharist makes fully explicit to us.

On the cross, as the representative of the Father who has seen the misery of his people, and who wishes to deliver them from the slavery of sin, he is the new Moses, who saves men by taking their place, when condemned to death, forsaken of God, and rejected by men. He is present in a still more wonderful way than that of the nativity. He is present as Saviour, making amends for our sins and giving us the love of the Father, associating us in his life: "I promise thee, this day shalt thou be with me in Paradise." This presence is that of the Father of all mercy, who sees the misery of his people, and makes use of their misery to come near them, to help them actively and effectively, by means of his omnipotence. He gives them

a new life. The resurrection of Christ shows us how far
the power of the almighty reaches. The effective presence
of love is real to the fullest extent.

This presence is only brought about for us in the
measure in which we wish to live in union with the heart
of Christ, in which we share the life of his loving worship
as Son, and of his love as the Good Shepherd giving his
life for his sheep. It is truly in our worship, in union with
that of Christ crucified, that we realize how he has been
given to us, how he is present, how God, through him
and in him, is present to us, as Father of all mercy, almighty in his mercy.

In this way we realize fully the mystery of the presence
of God to us and to the whole world. As the intimate
presence of the child Jesus at Bethlehem is an effective
symbol—a sacrament of the intimate presence of the
Father to Mary—the look of her child Jesus shows her
the love with which the Father looks upon her and upon
men, for this child, through Mary, is given to all souls of
good will, to all men who seek the love of God. So too,
the presence of the blood-stained Christ crucified on the
cross is an effective symbol—a sacrament of the power of
love, of mercy, of the Father's forgiveness to all men without exception, but especially to Mary, to John, to the holy
women. For the Lamb of God has borne the sins of all
men, the Lamb of God gives himself as the food of love
to all those who wish to live in his love. The omnipotence
of God, in the interests of love and mercy, bestows on the
cross a unique gift and a unique presence, that of the
Father welcoming his prodigal son, embracing him, and
forgiving him his sins. The reality is still greater than the
parable.

On the cross the presence of the Father to Jesus
crucified, to his beloved Son, brings about and manifests
the presence of the Father to men who are sinners. In the

presence of the Father the beloved Son is seen as the prodigal, so that the prodigal may live as a beloved son.

The mystery of the Eucharist, a mystery of presence, enables us to understand better this presence of the Father's love. When the Lord gave to his people the manna, a sign of the Eucharist, he said to Moses: "This be thy answer to the rebel talk I hear: This evening you shall have meat, and bread tomorrow to your hearts' content; will you doubt, then, that I am the Lord your God?" (Exod. 16. 12).

This mystery is the sacrament of the presence of the Father. It shows us how close and substantial is this presence. As Creator God is intimately present to all that exists, with a presence which is active and gives to everything its proper being and maintains it. The mystery of the Eucharist implies the miracle of transubstantiation: the substance of bread is changed into the substance of the body of Christ. This miracle is a sign of the full efficacy of God's word, which reaches the centre of all that is, and on which all that is wholly depends. God alone reaches in this way all that exists. Hence, to God the Creator there is no such thing as distance; all is open to his eyes. Creating by his word and by his *fiat:* "Let there be light; and the light began" (Gen. 1. 3), God sees all that is in his light—"darkness is no hiding-place from thee" (Ps. 138. 12). The close and clear contact of God with all that exists is necessarily direct, with no possible intermediary, for this would be contradictory to creative act. It is an act in which the creature cannot cooperate, for, in regard to this act, the creature is merely effect, and merely capacity. This presence of God as Creator is always the same, from the first creative act revealed at the beginning of Genesis to the last creative act of the last soul God will create. Such presence cannot increase, but exists absolutely, and lasts as long as God wills to maintain the creation. Every visible miracle of God is a sign of this presence, and manifests it. But, to the believer, the miracle of transubstantiation and of the resurrection of Christ's body are the plainest effects of the presence of the Creator in all that exists.[8]

The worship of Christ in the Eucharist in spirit and truth allows us to live in the presence of the almighty Creator. It makes us realize that God is our true home, and only refuge.

The Christian, however, cannot stop at the presence of the almighty Creator, however great and wonderful and clear it may be. The presence of the Creator should lead him on to realize the presence of the beloved Father's love and mercy, in which he can wholly lose himself, in loving worship.

Again, the mystery of the Eucharist is intended to give us a practical lesson. The miracle of the transubstantiation of the bread into the body of Jesus is directed towards the mystery of the Eucharist, the gift of Christ's body as a divine food. The Eucharist makes present to us the body of Christ, of the Lamb of God who suffered on the cross, of the Lamb glorified in heaven, by giving it to us as food. Plainly this presence and this gift are only for the children of God, the disciples of Christ, for those who believe in his word and in his merciful love. For him who believes in the word of Christ, the Eucharist is, thus, a presence of God through his gift of merciful love. God wills himself to feed his children; this is the manna, and he feeds them by giving himself as food, for the son of God can only be satisfied by God, by his Father. The Eucharist is the supreme sign of the fatherly presence of God's merciful love for each individual man. God is concerned with

[8] We must always distinguish carefully between the presence of God as Creator in all that exists, and the presence of God in the souls of the just by grace, which is the special presence of God to his people, to his beloved Son, and to those whom Jesus has redeemed on the cross, and feeds with his body.

fatherly care for each one; he knows all as the Good
Shepherd knows his sheep, he knows their sufferings, their
difficulties, and their struggles; he knows what is good in
each. He knows them as a friend knows his friend, with a
knowledge that is practical, affective and loving. He knows
them in order to help them and support them. Nothing
escapes his knowledge: God sees all. God can make use of
everything in order to help them. His omnipotence gives
complete efficacy to his fatherly care.

The sign of this care, to show how it is adapted for each
one, and full of tenderness, is the manna, the most excellent food, of every appetite the welcome choice.[9] One
person can only be fully present to another, to a friend,
when he has this tender care for him. Such care enables
us to act with a gentleness that is heartfelt. The fatherly
tenderness of God acts in this profound and peaceful way.
Hence the gift of the manna is the sign of a loving, watch-
ful presence.

This gift of bread expresses, too, how the presence of
love requires and effects union of life between God the
Father and the Son. The bread becomes the body of him
who feeds on it. When it is assimilated, it becomes identical with him who makes use of it. The Eucharist, which
gives us the body of Christ as food, shows us how Christ
wishes to unite us to him, to make us live with his life.
Unity of life should be brought about: "He who eats my
flesh, and drinks my blood, lives continually in me, and I
in him. As I live because of the Father, the living Father
who has sent me, so he who eats me will live, in his turn,
because of me" (John 6. 57–8).

[9] Wisd. 16. 20–1: "Them thou didst foster with the food of
angels; bread from heaven thou didst set before them, which no
labour of theirs had made ready, every taste uniting that could
bring content, of every appetite the welcome choice. So would thy
own nature manifest a father's universal love; this food should
humour the eater's whim, turning it into that which he craved
most."

This presence of love can only be compared to the presence of the Father in relation to that of his only Son. The presence of the Father to his Son is the presence of friend to friend in its deepest and most intimate element. Loving worship in spirit and truth, worship in union with that of the cross, in and through the mystery of the Eucharist, allows us, through faith, to live in this presence of love, of the infinitely tender care of the Father. Worship is then carried out in a filial confidence, in which we find how the merciful love of the Father surrounds us, supports us, feeds us, and transfigures us. By sin man can place an obstacle in the way of this presence of the Father's love for his children. Hence Scripture speaks of estrangement from God, of God's seeming to be absent, and no longer seeming to know where man is. These are metaphorical ways of speaking, to express the fact that man strays from God, and does not wish to turn lovingly towards him. In reality it is not God who departs from man, but it is man who of his own accord closes the gates of his soul and of his heart to the fatherly influence of God, and his merciful love.

When we speak of the presence of God as Creator, plainly this presence remains even after sin—for sin, while killing love, does not make the sinner cease to exist. He continues as an existing being, a wanderer, it is true, who has missed the path to his Father's house, but one who continues all the time to exist, and who lives in absolute dependence on his Creator. God as Creator cannot be driven from his creature, for the creature cannot annihilate itself, since its existence is not its own, but it belongs only to God. But God as Father, merciful love, Saviour of men, can be driven from man's heart by man himself, by his pride which will not accept this merciful love. Man cannot destroy in himself the traces of God as Creator, but he can destroy in his heart the loving and merciful fatherhood of his God.

THE SACRIFICE OF THE CROSS: THE REVELATION OF THE ETERNITY AND HOLINESS OF THE FATHER

O God, our Lord, what is your name? He tells us: my name is "he who is." What must I understand by "he who is"? That I live eternally, and cannot change. For things which change do not truly exist, because they do not remain what they are. That which is remains. That which changes has been one thing, and will be another, but does not truly exist, because it is changeable. Thus it is the divine immutability which has designed to reveal itself in the words "I am he who is." (St Augustine, *Sermo* 6, 3, 4.)

The years of God are not truly other than God himself; the years of God are the eternity of God; eternity is the very substance of God, in which nothing can be subject to change. In it nothing has passed in such a way as no longer to be; nothing is to come, as not yet being. In God, a single word, is; not, has been or will be; for that which has been no longer is, that which will be is not yet; and all that is in God, is, and cannot but be. (St Augustine, *Super Psalmos* 101. 11, 10.)

To worship God is in the first place to acknowledge the rights of the Creator over all that is. Worship in spirit and in truth implies that man offers to God what is dearest to him, not only the first-fruits of his labour, but his labour itself, his toil, in order to manifest to his own eyes, and before all human society, that he acknowledges that the whole value of his work comes from God, and that he can only cooperate in God's act. In this way man's labour can become a great liturgy of worship and promise, to the glory of God as Creator.

And, as the work of man—this way in which man co-operates with the world to transform it—gives to man an intense awareness of time, of the passing nature of his work, as well as of his dependence on time, and of his relative power of control over it, he can organize it as seems good to him; to offer his work to God implies the offering of his time. And this offering of time places us in the presence of the mystery of God's eternity. We can, for God's sake, consume the little time we have for living on earth, because God is eternal.

This mystery of God's eternity is one of the great attributes of God which we ought to consider more often in the present age, when we profess to find out the historical meaning of human follies and theories, and when we have such a clear awareness of the passing character of human affairs. Perhaps we are often in danger of assigning to these problems, which are undoubtedly very human and very important, a too absolute value, which gradually turns us away from the true absolute in the order of duration, that of eternity. For this reason it is very necessary for the believer often to return to the mystery of God's eternity, and, in the light of eternity, to gain a proper appreciation of human duration and its passing character. Scripture constantly speaks of God as the God of eternity (Gen. 1. 1), that is, as the God who will never pass away, as he who is the most ancient—(we cannot think of a being older than God)—as he who continues for ever.

Eternity means duration without end. A being with a beginning and an end cannot be eternal. A being with a beginning but continuing for ever is immortal, but not eternal. An eternal being is a being without any limitation in its duration. This, however, is only a negative definition of eternity. To be more accurate, we must say that an eternal being has duration without end and without succession, that is, fully and entirely, in a single instant. Therefore we can imagine eternity as an instant which lasts for ever, a substantial instant which never passes away, but is.

What we must bear in mind is that eternity is duration of supreme intensity, such that it can involve no succession. When we have joy of extraordinary intensity we can have some notion of what is represented by intensity in duration. This is only an image of eternity. When Scripture asserts that the Lord is an eternal God, obviously it does not explain itself fully, but rather helps us to have an idea of eternity by contrasting with its stability succession in time. Nevertheless, if we reflect on the assertion made so frequently, we are confronted with that characteristic which belongs to God's being, of which the duration is without limit, and which possesses itself perfectly without succession. Genesis begins by saying: "God, at the beginning of time, created heaven and earth." Hence God exists before the beginning of time in the universe, the earth, the heavens.

St Augustine emphatically expresses this contrast:

> Eternal and without beginning, yet he has given a beginning to time, and man, who had not yet been created, he made in time, not by a sudden, new, decision, but by an eternal and unchangeable plan. Who could fathom this unfathomable abyss, and know these impenetrable secrets? Who will say how God, without changing his will, created in time the man, subject to time, who was the first human being, and how from one alone, he has multiplied his race? For it is a profound mystery that God has always been, and that, in time, he has willed to create the first man, without changing his plan or his will. (St Augustine, *The City of God*, 12, 14.)

In the story of Abraham we are told that at Bersabee he called on the Lord God eternal (Gen. 21. 33).

At the end of the Bible, in the Apocalypse, God pre-

sents himself as one who contains and judges all generations: "I am Alpha, I am Omega, the beginning of all
things and their end, says the Lord God; he who is, and
ever was, and is still to come, the Almighty" (Apoc. 1. 8;
cf. 4. 8; 21. 6; 22. 13). God is also called he "who lives
for ever and ever" (Apoc. 4. 9). The twenty-four elders
worship him.

The conflict between the Lord, the eternal God, who
is before all creation, and who lives for ever, and the false
gods, the idols who live only for a time, is often declared
by the prophets. Moses first, in his canticle, emphasizes
this. Speaking of the infidelities of Jacob he says: "Not to
their God they offered sacrifice, but to devils, to gods yet
untried, upstart gods of yesterday, whom their fathers
never held in awe" (Deut. 32. 17). Idols are nothing:
"they can neither mar nor make thee." The lord alone is
"God in good earnest, a God that lives, that has eternal
dominion" (Jer. 10. 1–10).

The psalmist and the prophets also contrast the Lord
who lives for ever, and creatures who pass away, and only
live in time: "Like a tapering shadow my days dwindle,
wasting away, like grass in the sun. Lord, thou endurest
for ever, thy name, age after age, is not forgotten" (Ps.
101. 12–13). "Here, on my journey, he has brought
my strength to an end, cut short my days. What, my God,
wilt thou snatch me away, my life half done? Age after
age, thy years endure; it was thou, Lord, that didst lay
the foundation of earth when time began, it was thy hand
that built the heavens. They will perish, but thou wilt
remain; they will all be like a cloak that grows threadbare,
and thou wilt lay them aside like a garment, and exchange
them for new; thou art unchanging, thy years can never
fail" (Ps. 101. 24–8). "In thy sight, a thousand years are
but as yesterday, that has come and gone, or as one of the
night-watches. Swiftly thou bearest our lives away, as a

waking dream, or the green grass that blooms fresh with
the morning; night finds it faded and dead" (Ps. 89.
4–6). Speaking of the victories of the Lord, Isaias writes:
"Who was the author, the doer of all this, but I, the Lord,
who summon all the ages into being? Before all, and at
the end of all, I am" (Isaias 41. 4). "Mortal things are but
grass, the glory of them is but grass in flower; grass that
withers, a flower that fades, when the Lord's breath
blows upon it. . . . Grass that withers, a flower that
fades; but the word of our Lord stands for ever" (Isaias
40. 6–8).

"Naught that is, but God made it; he, the source of all
right, the King that reigns for ever unconquerable . . ."
(Ecclus. 18. 1–8).

The stability of the universe can also act as a means to
uplift us to the mystery of God's eternity: "He it was that
founded the solid earth, to abide immovable. Firm stood
thy throne ere ever the world began; from all eternity,
thou art" (Ps. 92. 1–2).

But, beyond these comparisons and contrasts, is proclaimed the mystery of the eternity of the Lord: "But the
Lord abides for ever on the throne of judgement he has
prepared" (Ps. 9. 8). "Lord, thou hast been our refuge
from generation to generation. Before the hills came to
birth, before the whole frame of the world was engen-
dered, from eternity to eternity, O God, thou art" (Ps.
89. 1–2). "Forget not, Lord, thy pity, thy mercies of long
ago" (Ps. 24. 6). "What ignorance is this? Has not the
rumour of it reached thee? This Lord of ours, who fashioned the remotest bounds of earth, is God eternally; he
does not weaken or grow weary; he is wise beyond all
thinking" (Isaias 40. 28). "None ever came into being
before me, or will after me. It is I, I, the Lord; no other
can bring deliverance . . . I am God, and what I was, I
am; from my power there is no escaping; when I execute

my designs, none can avert them" (Isaias 43. 10–13).
"All knowledge is his; does he not hold the clue of eternity, making plain what has been and what is yet to be,
laying bare the track of hidden things? . . . How great
the wisdom that so ordered all things, his wisdom who has
neither beginning nor end; nothing may be added, nothing taken away from them, nor needs he any man's counsel" (Ecclus. 42. 18–22). "Up, friends, and bless the
Lord your God, as blessed he must be from the beginning to the end of time! Blessed be thy glorious name, O
Lord, that is beyond all blessing and all praise!" (2
Esdras 9. 5).

In conclusion, we should notice the prayer of Jona-
than in the second book of Machabees, which expresses
so well the eternity promised to the children of God:

"Lord God, that all things madest, the terrible, the
strong, the just, the merciful, King gracious as none else;
none else so kindly, none else so just, as thou the almighty,
the eternal! Israel from all peril thou deliverest, thou didst
make choice of our fathers, and set them apart for thyself.
For the whole nation of Israel receive our sacrifice . . ."
(2 Mach. 1. 24–6).

The sacrifice of the seven brothers and their wonderful
mother is itself an appeal to eternal life. This sacrifice and
martyrdom is a living witness which declares the mystery
of the eternal life of God in God himself and in his elect.
Before his mystery of eternal life life in time is nothing.

The whole teaching of the New Testament consists in
the promise of eternal life, given to us by Christ himself,
who not only possessed in himself, as the Word and the
only Son of the Father, this eternal life, but is life eternal.

St John, in his prologue and throughout his Gospel,
constantly reveals to us the mystery of the eternal life of
the Word made flesh, and the importance of this mystery
for those who believe in him.

The first witness to the Word made flesh by John the Baptist, the messenger of God, is full of meaning:

"It is of him that I said, One is coming after me who takes rank before me; he was when I was not" (John 1. 30). Christ's first teaching, given to Nicodemus, a Jewish notable, a Pharisee, is plain: "And this Son of Man must be lifted up, as the serpent was lifted up by Moses in the wilderness; so that those who believe in him may not perish, but have eternal life. God so loved the world, that he gave up his only-begotten Son, so that those who believe in him may not perish, but have eternal life" (John 3. 14–16).

The final teaching of John the Baptist repeats that of Jesus, and is most emphatic: "He who believes in the Son possesses eternal life, whereas he who refuses to believe in the Son will never see life" (John 3. 36).

The final teaching of Jesus given to his disciples before his Passion is a prayer to his Father: "Father, the time has come; give glory now to thy Son, that thy Son may give glory to thee. Thou hast put him in authority over all mankind, to bring eternal life to all those thou hast entrusted to him. Eternal life is knowing thee, who art the only true God, and Jesus Christ, whom thou hast sent" (John 17, 1–3).

The mystery of the cross and of the resurrection, that is, the lifting up of the Son of Man foretold to Nicodemus, and the glorification of the Son prayed for to the Father, is indeed to the believer the great revelation of the mystery of eternity, of the eternal love of the Father, a revelation which is carried out through the gift of eternal life.

We should say still more exactly that the sacrificial martyrdom of the seven brothers and of their mother is a living witness showing that the will of the Father is eternal, that God himself, in his mystery, is beyond all succession, of generation and of time. Therefore, this eternal will can demand the offering up of our life in time in order to give us sooner eternal life. God wisely demands the sacrifice of a lesser reality for one that is higher, the sacrifice of earthly life for eternal life; anything else would be folly. Similarly, but in a higher way, the sacrificial martyrdom of Christ is a living witness showing that the loving will of the Father is eternal, that God himself, in his mystery of love, is beyond all change or alteration. The fact that Christ freely committed his soul into the hands of his Father proves that he acknowledged that his life in time, however splendid, was nothing in comparison to the eternal life of the Father. This was the life he longed for: "Father, do thou exalt me at thy own side, in that glory which I had with thee before the world began" (John 17. 5).

The martyrdom of Christ is thus the proof for us of the eternal life of the Father. Worshipping the Father, offering him his own life as a sacrifice of love, he bears witness that the life of the Father is more than all earthly life, that it is eternal life, able to make use of Christ's death to communicate to his human nature, to his dead body, a new, overflowing life, more perfect and divine than that which he had received from Mary.

The resurrection of Christ's body manifests and declares that this life received from the Father is an eternal life: "We know that Christ, now he has risen from the dead, cannot die any more; death has no more power over him." [10] In the Apocalypse the glorified Christ declares, "I, who underwent death, am alive, as thou seest, to endless ages, and I hold the keys of death and hell" (Apoc. 1. 18).

---

[10] Rom. 6. 9; cf. Acts 13. 34–5: "And this is how he describes raising him from the dead, never to return to corruption again, I will grant you the privileges I have promised to David; to which purpose he says in another psalm, Thou wilt not allow thy faithful servant to see corruption." Cf. 1 John 10; Heb. 2. 14 fol.; Ps. 16. 10.

To assert that the life of the Father is eternal life is to assert that this life has no need of increase in order to exist perfectly, that it has no need of modification. It is a perfect life, which possesses in itself, in complete immanence, all the perfection of life. Eternal life is a life which will not change, but not through weakness or lack of energy; it is a life which will not change, and cannot change, because it is so perfect that it has in itself all the fullness of life. God alone is eternal life, because God alone subsists in his own being, his own life. Being eternal life he is the source of all life. For this reason he is able to make use of Christ's death, as of that of the seven brothers and their mother, to communicate to the body of Christ, as to the bodies of the seven brothers and their mother, when he wills, a new, overflowing life, a real participation in eternal life, and consequently a life victorious over all death.

The martyrdom of Christ, being the martyrdom of the beloved Son, of him who is faithful to the end, proves in a special way that the love of the Father is eternal love, which knows no change, a love which remains always the same, which is faithful. God is eternal in his love, he is supremely faithful.[11]

By declaring that God possesses eternal life, that his love is eternal, we declare at the same time that God, in his very being, is eternal, that he lives in eternity. Hence, in our changing, corruptible world, the cross of Jesus is truly the sacrament of God's eternity, the sign which is given in the last days to show that God's eternity alone remains. This sign is the way leading us to the mystery of God's eternity. By means of the cross we can live the eternal life of God. This eternal life is given us; God's eternal love is

---

[11] Cf. Deut. 7. 9: "And thou wilt find it ever the same; the Lord thy God is God Almighty, is God ever faithful; if men will love him and keep his commandments, he is true to his word, and shews mercy to them while a thousand generations pass."

given us. By means of the cross an opening is made through the succession of human generations, and of time, and the mystery of God's eternity, of eternal life, of eternal love, can be caught sight of. It is communication to us by faith, if we so desire.

The sacrifice of the cross brings us, therefore, near to the eternal God. It enables us to share in his eternal life and love, and understand how this mystery of eternity contains in a higher way all the riches spread throughout time. The eternity of God contains in a unity of life and love, in perfect simplicity, all that is effected gradually through successive generations.

The sacrifice of the cross also brings us near to the holiness of God. We cannot worship God without finding out and acknowledging his holiness; and recognition of God's holiness calls for worship.

It is interesting to call to mind how God has gradually revealed to us his holiness, and how man has gradually acknowledged it and worshipped it. Here just a few aspects of this revelation may be mentioned, to give a better understanding how the sacrifice of the cross puts us in the presence of the loving holiness of the Father and of that of the whole Trinity.

The first time that Scripture speaks of holiness is during the incident of the burning bush. Moses, astonished at the sight of the bush on fire, which was not consumed, decided to approach "to see more of it", and to see why this bush was not consumed. God called to him from the midst of the bush: "Moses, Moses; and when he answered, I am here, at thy command, he was told, Do not come nearer; rather take the shoes from thy feet, thou art standing on holy ground" (Exod. 3.3–5).

The presence of the Lord in the bush made the place holy ground, that is, ground consecrated to God, which it was wrong to defile with impunity. The need to take off his shoes meant that he must purify himself in order to approach God, to approach the place where God was found, because God is holy.

Everything that is near to God, that is consecrated to him, is to be considered holy. The most secret and hidden place in the temple is to be consecrated to God, and called the Holy of Holies. Not only certain places, but also certain days are to be consecrated to him; the Sabbath is to be the Lord's day, and must be kept holy (Exod. 20. 8–11): "Keep my sabbath; it has a binding claim on you, on pain of death for all who violate it" (Exod. 31. 14).

The ark is regarded as consecrated to the Lord. It is holy. Profane persons cannot touch it without dying (2 Kings 6. 6–7). All objects used in the great liturgy of the temple are regarded as consecrated and holy. Speaking of the tabernacle, the ark, the table with its appurtenances, the lampstand, the altar used for incense and that used for burnt-sacrifice, the Lord commanded Moses: "All these thou shalt sanctify, and they shall be all holiness; whoever touches them shall become holy thereby" (Exod. 30. 29). The oil used for anointing was to be considered holy, "a thing you must keep set apart for me, age after age" (Exod. 30. 31). The offerings made to the Lord were also holy things, set apart for God, and, in a certain sense, for the priests (Numb. 18. 9).

Then there were persons who were holy and consecrated to God: all Israel, and especially the priests, who belonged to God (Exod. 19. 6). Israel must not worship idols, since they were a people consecrated to the Lord, who was their God. They were the people of the Lord (Deut. 7. 6). And, speaking of the sons of Aaron, the Lord said, "They are men set apart for their God, and must never bring reproach on his name; they burn incense to the Lord, offer their God his consecrated loaves, and shall they not be holy?" (Lev. 21. 6).

The Lord himself explained why all that is concerned with him, all that is consecrated to him, is holy; it is because he himself is holy. Speaking of priests he commands: "they must be set apart, as I, the Lord, am set apart, the Lord that hallows them" (Lev. 21. 8).

Holiness is one of the great attributes of the Lord, perhaps the supreme attribute, which he reveals to his people in the Old Testament, for it is the principal attribute which governs every action of religion: "I am the Lord your God; you must be set apart, the servants of a God who is set apart . . . I am the Lord your God, who rescued you from the land of Egypt; I am set apart and you must be set apart like me" (Lev. 11. 44–6). "You must be men set apart, as I am set apart" (Lev. 19. 2). "You must be set apart for my service, as I am set apart, I, your God, who have chosen you out among all the nations of the world, to belong to me" (Lev. 20. 26). "Do not dishonour my holy name; it is among the sons of Israel that I would vindicate my holiness, I, the Lord, who have set you apart for myself' (Lev. 22. 32).

This need for holiness, on account of the holiness of God, which is at the heart of the whole covenant of Mount Sinaï, was soon to take on a legal aspect—legal holiness. Thus the prophets did not cease to call to mind that holiness is principally an inward attitude of the heart and of the will, for the holiness of God is the holiness of a Person, not of a Law.

The prophet Isaias does not cease to declare the holiness of God: "Woe to a sinful nation, a people bowed with guilt, a rebellious race, a brood foully degenerate. They have forsaken God, they have spurned the Holy One of Israel, turned strangers to me" (Isaias 1. 4). "Doom, by which the Lord of hosts will be exalted, just award, by which the God of holiness will shew holier yet" (Isaias 5. 16).

In his great vision of the Lord the prophet sees Seraphim before the throne of the Lord, each with six wings, two to veil his face, two to cover his feet, two to fly, who cried out: "Holy, holy, holy, is the Lord God of hosts; all the earth is full of his glory" (Isaias 6. 3). "He who is our light will turn into a fire, the Holy One of Israel will be a flame, that will burn up suddenly; in one day those thorn-bushes, that dry brushwood shall be consumed. Like a proud forest, or a garden plot, he shall be eaten up, body and soul; see where he flies in terror" (Isaias 10. 17–18).

Here the holiness of God explains the power of justice against the king of Assyria. But, in regard to his people, reduced to nothing after the exile, the Holy One of Israel is full of mercy: "I am here, says the Holy One of Israel, to ransom thee" (Isaias 41. 14).

In revealing himself as the Holy One, the Lord expresses his absolute transcendence. He is the One who is set apart from all that is created, who cannot be touched by that which is created. He cannot be profaned. He is pure throughout his whole being, his whole life, his whole love. There is nothing impure in him. God cannot enter into composition with what he is not. He is set apart. Hence all that is consecrated to him is taken from ordinary, profane use. All that is consecrated to him must be pure.

The holiness of God does not only mean that God is set apart from all that is profane, but also that he is set apart from all sin. Hence sin is utterly opposed to God's holiness.

When, however, God declares that he is holy, when the prophets, and especially the prophet Osee, proclaims his holiness, more is asserted than this negative aspect of being set apart; it is also asserted that the Lord, because he is holy, is able to forgive through love and to sanctify whom he wills, to consecrate them, and keep them for himself. Thus the holiness of God implies a high and overwhelming jealousy, able to attract and determine without any rival.

It is this aspect of God's holiness which Christ specially reveals to us in a new way during his earthly life, and above all in the mystery of the cross.

As a result of the mystery of the hypostatic union he has a human nature, wholly consecrated to God. He is the anointed of God, holy in all his being, in all his human nature (Heb. 7. 26). Hence he can manifest to us in a special way the mystery of God's holiness, the mystery of the Father's holiness. Our Lord told his disciples to address the Father in this way: "Hallowed by thy name (Matt. 6. 9; Luke 11. 2–4).

In his great prayer as a priest Jesus calls on the holiness of the Father: "Holy Father, keep them true to thy name, thy gift to me, that they may be one, as we are one" (John 17. 11). It is the holiness of the Father which draws those whom he loves with such jealousy as to unite them with himself, in a union like that which exists between the heavenly Father and his beloved Son. And Jesus adds: "I dedicate myself for their sakes, that they too may be dedicated through the truth" (John 17. 19).

In his sacrifice on the cross Jesus crucified, a holy victim, making amends for sin, glorifies the holiness of the Father and hallows his name—the fulfilment of what the Lord declared through his prophet: "That great renown of mine I mean to vindicate that is now dragged in the dust because of you. The very Gentiles will recognize my power, the Lord God says, when I proclaim my majesty in their sight by delivering you" (Ezech. 36. 23).

He reveals to us how the Father is set apart from all sin, how sin opposes his love. He reveals to us how the Father wishes to forgive, to cleanse all who are sorry for their sins. The whole human race can be perfectly cleansed, through the sacrificed Lamb. He reveals to us how the Father desires to consecrate, not only his own people, but all men, by a new covenant, a holy covenant in the Blood and Body of his Son. In the Blood of his Son the Father creates all men anew; he creates them anew in the image of his beloved, only, Son, in whom he is well pleased; he creates them anew by uniting them to his Son as living members of a single Body, sharing in the life of the Son, living by his Spirit of love. Thus the Father unites men to himself in an utterly new way, and carries out the prayer of his Son: "Holy Father . . . that they may be one as we are one." Here is the fruit of his overflowing holiness, which draws all jealously to himself. It is on the cross, in and through his crucified Son, that he draws all men, that he draws them and consecrates them in love which will have no rival.

The sacrifice of the cross reveals to us the threefold holiness of God, that of the Father, the Son and the Spirit: "Holy, holy, holy, is the Lord God, the Almighty, who ever was, and is, and is still to come" Apoc. 4. 8); the holiness of being set apart, the holiness of purification and of light, the holiness of unity and consecration. By revealing to us the holiness of the Father, he reveals to us his own holiness as beloved Son, in whom the Father is well pleased, and he gives to us his Spirit, the Holy Ghost.

The calling of the Christian is, therefore, a calling to holiness: "It is a holy God who has called you, and you too must be holy in all the ordering of your lives; you must be holy, the Scripture says, because I am holy" (1 Peter 1. 15–16).

CONCLUSION

Including, as it does, all the perfections of the Old Testament sacrifices, and going beyond them, the sacrifice of the cross is indeed for the Christian the wisdom of God, a wisdom which allows him to worship, in spirit and in truth, the one God, his Creator and his Father. It is a wisdom which allows him to contemplate and glorify all the splendours of his God and of his Father. The whole revelation of the Old Testament, concerning the mystery of God and of his attributes, is truly fulfilled on the cross. The cross puts us in the presence of the God who is thrice holy and one, eternal, almighty, all-seeing, present to everything that exists, just and merciful, infinitely good, simple. What had been revealed only partially and in outline is at once clearly manifested. In the presence of the cross man cannot remain indifferent. The three attitudes described by St Paul always remain true.

> To those who court their own ruin, the message of the cross is but folly; to us, who are on the way to salvation, it is the evidence of God's power. So we read in scripture, I will confound the wisdom of wise men, disappoint the calculations of the prudent. What has become of the wise men, the scribes, the philosophers of this age we live in? When God shewed us his wisdom, the world, with all its wisdom, could not find its way to God; and now God would use a foolish thing, our preaching, to save them who will believe in it. Here are the Jews asking for signs and wonders, here are the Greeks intent on their philosophy; but what we preach is Christ crucified; to the Jews, a discouragement, to the Gentiles, mere folly; but to us who have been called, Jew and Gentile alike, Christ the power of God, Christ the wisdom of God. (1 Cor. 1. 18–24.)

The cross is folly to the Gentiles, discouragement to the Jews, wisdom to the believer. We have experienced these three attitudes strongly in ourselves, and can do so again. That is natural. For the Gentile is the philosopher who reasons, and there is always a philosopher in each of us who reasons, and wishes to judge everything by his own standard. He always finds that the mystery of the cross is folly, and absurdity, and that he should consider this meaningless "fact" as little as possible. He should disregard it, and try to explain the world as it presents itself to us; he should try to explain man as we experience him in ourselves and round about us. The philosopher of this kind could accept God as the Creator, as the first being, and omnipotent; he could agree to worship him within himself, while declaring his dignity and rights as Creator. Often, however, he stops here. The acts of worship performed by Abel and Noe, if accepted, are regarded as primitive symbols of this spiritual worship directed to the one Creator and God. True worship, "in spirit and in truth," that of Christ crucified, he cannot accept, for he does not grasp the true demands of divine love, a love of friendship, a jealous and personal love. He does not enter into the mystery of faithfulness, which alone gives meaning to the sacrifice of the cross. It is not foolish or absurd to acknowledge that God is love, and that, in his jealous love, God demands the inward sacrifice of our way of judging. He demands the sacrifice of obedience so that his love may be able to have free play. The philosopher who at the present day has such a high regard for freedom, can still admit the free worship of a spirit turning to him who is the Creator of the world, but he is opposed to a worship which takes the humble form of obedience, and which expressed a love which, in order to be faithful, is willing to lose its splendour, worship of the Crucified, of him who is despised, rejected of men, of him who obeys the Father.

The worship of the cross always remains folly to the philosopher. We must not try to humanize the cross, so as to make it more acceptable to the philosopher, for then we get rid of the mystery. We must agree that the cross is only wisdom to the believer, and we must recognize that it is, and always will be, a mystery for our reason. We cannot confine the mystery of God within the limits of our reason. If this mystery is present to us fully, it is not surprising that our poor reason should be wholly out of its depth.

We ourselves have perhaps experienced the mystery of the cross as a discouragement. To the man of sensibility, who lives by his feelings, the worship of Christ crucified is not merely unbearable, but is a scandal, a stone of stumbling, which holds him back and makes him fall. The mystery of the cross has the appearance of opposing the instinctive tendencies of our sensibility and our ideals. Nothing seems less natural to us. Nothing seems so violent, so anti-human. If we let our human heart speak in accordance with its feelings and tendencies, it will always avoid taking into consideration the demands involved in the sacrifice of the cross. We may have a religious sense on the level of sensibility, which leads us to religious practices, which makes us love an attitude of devotion and prayer, but such a religious sense is scandalized by the mystery of the cross. If it claims to love God, this is really for the sake of the sensible, human delight experienced in some liturgical ceremony. A religious sense of this kind may of course assume very different forms, ranging from the romantic feelings of one who is moved by the smoke of incense and the atmosphere of a particular place of worship, to the refined, aesthetic sense of the artist in religious matters, who loves a beautiful ceremony, or the impressive sound of Gregorian chant. It may, on the other hand, be the path to a truer and deeper practice of religion though, if it is confined within the man himself, it will never reach a real act of worship, directed to the God who is Creator.

If the philosopher, as such, cannot get beyond a worship which looks to God as Creator, the man who remains in this state of religious feeling cannot get beyond an image which he makes for himself of God. It is not surprising that he is discouraged by the reality of the sacrifice of the cross, which reaches out to God in his mystery of inward, jealous love. Here again we must not try to reduce the true God to the images, dreams and artistic ideas which we imagine. We must accept the fact that we cannot directly reach the one God through our imagination and artistic appreciation.

We must recognize that faith alone in Christ crucified allows us to reach God in his personal mystery, in his mystery of merciful, just love, in his mystery of almighty, eternal love, and allows us to share the life of this mystery of God's love, given and communicated to us through filial worship of Jesus.

Such faith does not destroy our reason and understanding; quite the opposite, it intensifies our spiritual love, letting it become more itself. It is through loving God with supernatural, divine love, together with Christ crucified, that we have a true love of ourselves, and of those who are around us. Such love can possess the highest power and deepest feeling, for it unites our hearts closely to the source of all love.

Our artistic appreciation is itself cleansed and strengthened, for it finds itself ennobled from within by the living faith which unites it to him who is the masterpiece of God, to him who, in his mystery of the cross and in his mystery of the resurrection, is truly the Glory of the Father.

Worship of Christ crucified is indeed to the believer the wisdom of God. It alone carried to their fulfilment the different acts of worship of the Old Testament; it alone leads us directly to the Kingdom of God, to the contemplation of his mystery and of his attributes.

SELECT BIBLIOGRAPHY

In this series: *What is the Trinity?*
What is Faith?
The God of Reason.
What is the Bible?

AUGUSTINE, St: *Confessions,* translated by F. J. Sheed, London and New York, Sheed and Ward, 1949.

DANIÉLOU, Jean, S.J.: *God and Us,* London, Mowbray, 1957; American edition: *God and the Ways of Knowing,* New York, Meridian Books, 1957.

GARRIGOU-LAGRANGE, Reginald, O.P.: *God: His Existence and His Nature,* St. Louis, Mo., Herder, Volume 1, 1934, Volume 2, 1936; *One God,* St. Louis, Mo., Herder, 1943.

HENRY, A. M., O.P.: *God and His Creation,* Volume 2 in The Theology Library, Cork, Mercier Press and Chicago, Fides, 1956.

SHEED, F. J.: *Theology and Sanity,* London and New York, Sheed and Ward, 1947.